COMMON Wildflowers OF SPAIN

Austen F. Colwell

SANTANA BOOKS

Common Wildflowers of Spain

Published by Ediciones Santana, S.L.
Apartado 41
29650 Mijas-Pueblo (Málaga)
Spain

Tel.: (0034) 952 48 58 38
Fax: (0034) 952 48 53 67
E-Mail: info@santanabooks.com
Website: www.santanabooks.com

Designed by Chris Fajardo

Printed in Spain by Gráficas San Pancracio, S.L.

ISBN: 978-84-89954-72-4
Depósito Legal: MA-485/2008

For my wife Molly and family and especially for my grandchildren, Lilly, George, Peter and Jaime. For my lifelong friend, plants-man and author Kenneth A. Beckett. To my late friend and colleague Dennis Smith, who had the confidence to suggest the original idea. And for the happy people of Andalucía.

And for the brave parents, Aberfran.

"I know a bank where the wild thyme blows,
Where oxlips and the nodding violet grows,
Quite over-canopied with luscious woodbine,
With sweet musk roses and with eglantine."

ACKNOWLEDGEMENTS

I am indebted and extremely grateful to the following for their kind assistance in preparing this book.

Kenneth A. Beckett, for helping to identify and confirm the identification of certain plants.

Per Furu, for proof-reading and assistance with the computer.

Professor Gerald Wiener, for assisting with the computer, and likewise to my daughter Sally.

Carlos Ocaña Medina, for lending his support and company during my long plant forays in the mountains.

Maurice W. Matthews, for the photographs of biarum and mandragora.

Alan and Gertrude Roberts, for their patience and confidence. David Baird for his editing and Chris Fajardo for his designing expertise in preparing the book.

My grateful thanks to the staff of the photographic department at El Corte Inglés in Fuengirola for their patient help in locating, recording and viewing many photographic images and also to the proprietor of the 'local' Inspirations at Mijas-Costa for his assistance and professional advice.

CONTENTS

ABOUT THIS GUIDE

THIS guide is designed to allow the beginner, the casual observer or the amateur plant man to readily identify plants. For this reason it departs from the norm, the plants being arranged in simple alphabetical Common Name order rather than formal Natural Order or Family Grouping of Plants, general to classical scientific plant textbooks. However, the scientific or Latin name is included, next to the Common Name. Latin Natural Order names, or Family Names, are included in the descriptions of each plant. At the end of the guide you will find a list of English names alongside their Latin and common Spanish equivalents.

Persons interested and perhaps to some extent familiar

with the Common Names but with limited knowledge of scientific nomenclature should be able to recognise a plant from its illustration, verifying this if necessary from the text. A method one hopes which may lead the casual observer to a greater understanding and knowledge of the wild flora and possibly stimulate an even greater interest.

To some extent Common Names are unreliable, thus the bluebell of Scotland is the harebell of England, but this is an extreme example. Most Common Names are linked to a characteristic of the plant. Some possess a Latin name only.

Most of the plants portrayed are common and may be spied without much effort. Many may be seen from the road. In some areas bright yellow wattles create a winter delight. Oleanders and Spanish broom colour roadsides bright yellow and pink or white in May. Christmas iris may easily be spotted, for example, in Málaga province on the road to Ronda via the villages of Monda, Guaro, Alozaina and Yunquera. But to see other flowers will require a walk along country tracks and, to view more specialised plants, take a trip to the sparkling air of the Spanish sierras.

All the plant images are taken in situ in the wild, the intention being to illustrate a plant so that it should be more-or-less immediately recognisable from the portrait alone. For keener readers, the texts, though brief, should provide an exact identification as effort has been made to include the plants' diagnostic characters. Above all, the guide is intended to afford an enjoyable experience, even if one does nothing more than view the colour portraits.

— A. F. Colwell, 2008

INTRODUCTION

PLANT SPOTTING

A fair number of the plants contained within the guide may be spotted in the local park, a garden, sometimes even in a window box or a hanging basket. Hard to believe? No, if one is able to recognise seedling plants. Just recently the author removed young horehound plants from a hanging basket and discovered the beautiful but so invasive Bermuda buttercup invading pot plants. Usually most plants such as these are removed well before they have time to mature and flower. Nevertheless, a number, especially the quick-growing annuals in the garden or park, may reach the flowering stage, such as the scarlet pimpernel, groundsel, various thistles, sow thistles, dandelions, poppies, including the opium poppy, to name a few.

Wall pellitory, ivy-leaved toadflax, shepherd's purse and even coarse large-leaved henbane thrive on neglected walls and pavements. Duck weed, water lilies and other aquatic plants often find a home in the local park ponds and lakes. The key is observation.

Naturally, many plants are restricted to fallow or cultivated country fields, in olive groves, vineyards, scrub woodlands, fields, marshes, bogs, ditches, streams, riversides, hills and mountains. For those who live on or near the Costa del Sol, a walk through the hills around the villages of Guaro in February, March, April and May will reveal many varied, colourful plants. Such plants as orchids may be found along tracks near the village of Monda and near such towns as Coín, Estación de Cártama or Alhaurín el Grande.

For more specialised plants it may be necessary to travel further, to Grazalema, the wettest area in Andalusia, to the cork oak woods of western Spain and to the marshes of the Doñana National Park. Close to San Roque, in the province of Cádiz, you can find the small, autumn-flowering green narcissus. To the east, the very dry areas of Murcia possess their own special flora. Portugal sports the highly attractive, over-gathered, February-flowering *Narcissus cyclamineus*. The list is extensive and even more so when we take to the hills and mountains, a wild plant paradise in outstandingly beautiful scenic surrounds.

Even so, not all mountains are conducive to plant life, some remaining practically barren due to rock and soil conditions, height or lack of water and some, such as the upper parts of the Sierra Nevada, being too high to sustain plant life. It is the mountains of northern Spain which provide the richest botanical treasure trove. The grand scenic splendour of the Pyrenees and the Cantabrian mountains is the setting for a great variety of plant life. But take care to venture forth on mountain forays when the weather is set fair. These mountains may be tranquil and beautiful on fine days, but they can cloud over with amazing rapidity, presenting unsuspected perils.

One particularly worthwhile drive in the north follows the road that snakes up from Covaleda in Soria province to the Laguna Negra de Urbión, then along a forest road up to the Puerto de Santa Inés, 1,753 metres above sea-level and on the edge of the Rioja region. Along this route one may see as late as June such plant gems as wild tulips, dwarf narcissi, dog's tooth violet, pinguiculas and orchids in abundance, to mention but a few. Snow lurks on the heights and may still be deep in some corries as late as August.

The Pyrenees, the central sierras and the eastern block all boast floras distinct, even endemic, to their area. Spring is the ideal season to visit Extremadura, lakes and reservoirs north of the central meseta and the Sierra Morena — the road from Pozoblanco north through the Valle de Alcudia passing over the river Guadalmez near the village of San Benito possesses many fine plants with easy access. Flowers brightly colour the fields and sierras of Andalusia from March to June. And in coastal areas you will find special plants around cliffs, salt shores and marshes, seashore sands and dunes.

So much to see, and so much more than this small guide can mention. Even so, one hopes the appetite and interest of the holder may well be whetted.

POISONOUS PLANTS

A number of plants referred to possess poisonous properties, a few extremely poisonous. Handling poisonous plants poses no risk, providing they are not tasted or eaten, although taken in properly prescribed medicinal doses some poisons are positively beneficial, e.g. foxglove *(Digitalis purpurea)* or the highly poisonous and narcotic deadly nightshade *(Atropa belladona)*. Washing one's hands immediately after handling is recommended as a means of alleviating any unlikely problem. Historically, it seems very few people appear to have been adversely affected by either handling or eating poisonous plants, except those unfortunate enough to have allergies to certain plants or those who consumed poisonous fungi.

One plant which, when it occurs in Britain, raises great alarm, especially in the media, is the highly poisonous thorn apple *(Datura stromonium)*. One wonders why. Is it because, unlike deadly nightshade, it surfaces among urban populations or because the fruit supposedly resembles an apple (an apple

densely clad in unattractive, green, blunt spines, rather like a sweet chestnut husk). In Spain, however, the plant's frequent presence arouses no particular interest.

HONEY BEES, POLLINATION AND PLANT HYBRIDISATION

A recent alarm suggesting the possible demise of the honey bee and the probable adverse effects on man gives extra significance to the following account of pollination problems.
A plant-breeding station had the task of breeding a new top-quality hardy cauliflower from two available plants. One was a very small, curded but hardy, almost non-culinary variety, the other with large, soft but frost-tender curds. The requirement: to breed hardiness into the large tender variety without loss of size and to improve quality still further, if possible.

Accordingly, the cauliflowers were planted inside a huge polythene tunnel, the soft-curded variety on one side and the hardy small-curded on the other. Nothing to do now but culture the plants until they flowered. Which they did, but one three weeks before the other.

The following year the plants were planted again, except this time proper steps were taken to ensure they flowered simultaneously, and so they did, profusely. Now to introduce the bee hives. But yet again, disaster. Honey bees are selective and favoured one plant only, completely ignoring the other. So the desired cross was delayed yet another year.

Now what to do? Cross-pollination by hand would be far too expensive and the introduction of bumble bees, well known to be excellent non-selective plant pollinators had impossible practical difficulties. Even so the plants were planted as before and the necessary time-flowering device put into action.

The following spring each variety bloomed to perfection at exactly the right time, but still the problem: how to effect the cross. The answer proved relatively simple. Hundreds of blow-flies were introduced into the tunnel and as they flitted from flower to flower they unwittingly brought about the desired cross-pollination.

Since hearing this story I admit to having much greater consideration for the common blowfly, or bluebottle, than had previously.

LAND MASS CLIMATE, SOILS, FORESTS AND PLANTS

Spain's flora is vast, considered to be the most extensive in Europe. There are well over 2,500 known, named plants in the Mediterranean area alone. It also boasts a land mass almost three and a half times that of the size of Britain. It comes therefore as no great surprise that in climate it varies greatly, from temperate in the north to semi-tropical along the Mediterranean coast. Between there exist many variations, from macro to micro-climates, all playing their part in plant habitat selection. Temperatures inland are extreme, hot as hell in summer, freezing in winter. Spring and autumn afford welcome relief. More rain falls on the western flank, while semi-desert conditions prevail in some parts of Almería and Murcia.

Great oak and pine forests still exist, though many suffer even today from the depredations brought about by building great vessels for the Spanish Armada. At that time, the strength and particularly the shape of timber for ship construction was of paramount importance. Because carpenters couldn't bend and work timber as they do today, most of the finest trees were destroyed simply to obtain a special shape. More importantly, perhaps, their progeny was lost, too. Inferior trees and plants give rise to similar inferior stock.

Apart from its forests, Spain has an amazing variety of cultivated plants. Fine wines are produced from vineyards in almost every region. Galicia and Asturias are renowned for their pastoral products, Valencia for its oranges and olive trees clothe more than half the southern part of the peninsula.

Soils vary widely. Fertile soils along the coastal plains combine with ambient temperatures and favourable climate, permitting intensive horticulture. Many commercial plants form a monoculture, perhaps the most spectacular being the extensive fields of sunflowers (Helianthus annuus). Intensive plant culture in polythene tunnels covering endless expanses may be ugly and boring but nature is not to be outdone. Spring brings colourful wild flora to decorate fields, hillsides, hedges and roadsides with masses of scarlet poppies, pink and white cistus, cream and gold chrysanthemums, purple buglosses and such delightful plants as peonies.

Weather is greatly influenced by the mountains that rise steeply from the coastal plains (the southern mountains, considered young in geological terms, are still rising at the rate of one metre every thousand years). Huge plateaus and deep basins cover much of the central massif while bears and a few of Europe's remaining wolves roam remote areas. The special geographical conditions combine to create great rainfall, wind and weather variations; El Cabo de Gata receives an average annual rainfall of 122mm, Santiago de Compostela 1655mm, Málaga 600mm, Valencia 472mm, Barcelona 526mm and Sevilla 500mm. Small wonder then that the Iberian peninsula contains such an extensive and varied flora. Sadly, development has taken its toll (we all need somewhere to live). However, on the credit side, Spain possesses some excellent national parks, providing a haven for flaura and fauna alike.

One hopes this small guide will give the reader an initial insight into, and a greater awareness of, the abundance, variety and colour offered by the flora of Spain.

IDENTIKIT FOR PLANT PARTS

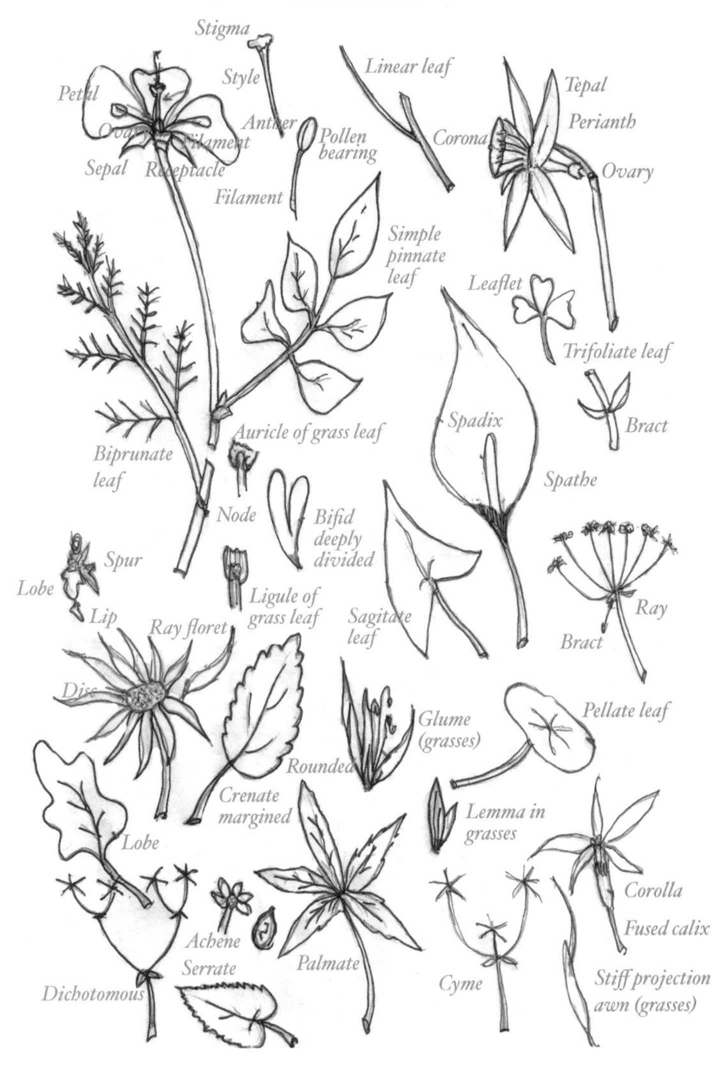

A to Z of plants

Note: *Common names capitalised, generic names in small letters.*

13.04.09 BARBATE ~ DE LA BREÑA (P)

AARON'S ROD

Verbascum thapsus

A tall, striking, architecturally statured, biennial mullein, up to 2m high, sometimes annual. Covered throughout in soft cream-grey white. Wool, softly pleasing to the touch, felt-like hair. Basal leaves in the primary year strongly rosetted and adpressed. Very large, oval-oblong short-stalked with narrow wings. Leaves reducing up the stem in flowering, then to become decurrent almost leaf to leaf. Flowers up to 35mm wide, cup-shaped, primrose yellow, borne in densely flowered, long, stately, broad, strong spikes. Stamen filaments five, the three above white hairy, the two below usually hairless.

Habitat: dry open areas, on banks, roadsides, old walls and bridges, rocky areas, sparse grass and roadsides, Spain, southern Europe and UK.

Family: Scrophulariaceae.

AEGILOPS

Aegilops ovatus

A distinctive low, fast-growing annual grass, bearing dark, rounded, long, spiky awned heads up to 30cm high. Heads few, more-or-less ovate, spikelets two to five. Awns two to five, up to 5cm long, stiff, pale green to straw colour, outward spreading. Leaves sparse in number, triangular, shorter than the ligules.

Habitat: Common throughout the Mediterranean, on road and track sides, arid wastelands, dry sandy banks and fields.

Family: Gramineae.

AEONIUM

Aeonium arboreum

Perennial, fleshy sub-shrub, readily recognised by its thick stout softly woody stems, branching into low tree-like form, leafless below. Leaves spatular-shaped, ends triangular, pale shiny green, sometimes tinged dull red or purple, terminating the branches in close, flat, spirally arranged rosettes. Individual flowers daisy-like, petals separate, nine to eleven, bright yellow tinged light green, borne conspicuously in large cone-like panicles.
Habitat: Native to Morocco. A handsome plant when in flower, widely cultivated and naturalised throughout the Mediterranean coast.
Family: Crassulaceae.

ALEXANDERS

Smyrmium olusatrum

Robust, pungent, biennial branching herb up to 150cm high, stems furrowed, upper branches usually opposite. Leaves stalked, large ternately lobed, serrated, dark green, grading yellow green upwards. Upper leaves smaller than those below, opposite, less divided (simple ternate). Flowers dense in rounded axillary terminal, yellow-green, seven to 15 rayed umbels, borne on short pedicels. Edible plant.
Habitat: Widespread throughout the Mediterranean and Europe, naturalised in the UK. Local, in damp places, hedgerows, cliffs, streams and near the sea.
Family: Umbellifereae.

BRIXHAM!!

ALKANET

Anchusa azurea

A tall, bristly, hairy perennial, up to 1m high, at once conspicuous for its beautiful bright blue flowers borne on open lax branching flower heads. Stems broad, erect, hairy, winged. Leaves, lanceolate, lower-stalked reducing upwards becoming stem-clasping. Flowers up to 2.5cm across, petals rounded, sky-blue with white hair central boss, all borne in loose heads topping the plant. Non-fragrant, but when dried the leaves possess a light pleasant odour.
Habitat: Common throughout the Mediterranean, on track and roadsides, banks, fallow and cultivated fields and waste areas. Tends to grow solitary or in small groups.
Family: Boraginaceae

ALMOND

Prunus dulcis

A fairly well-known flowering tree, up to 10m high, cultivated commercially for its fruits and ornamentally for its flowers. Leaves hairless, bright green, short-stalked bearing two very small glands, lanceolate, serrate. Flowers borne before the leaves, large, appealing, to 5cm wide, white or pink, fragrant. Fruits quickly maturing, husks large, grey-green ellipsoid, ends recurved. Nuts light brown very hard, oval, deeply crinkled. Mainly two varieties, sweet or bitter, the bitter variety possessing minute traces of bitter-tasting prussic acid.
Habitat: Common throughout the Mediterranean orchards, making a fine late winter, white or pink display. Widely cultivated in Europe. An escape into rocky areas, thickets and roadsides, usually close to cultivations.
Family: Rosaceae.

ALPINE ERINUS
Erinus alpinus

Low, many-stemmed glabrous or hairy alpine perennial up to 15cm high. Leaves opposite or alternate. Lower rosetted, linear elliptic to spathulate, short-stalked and narrowed at the base, wavy-edged, lightly toothed or entire. Flowers terminal in loose spikes, five petalled, two smaller and narrower than the opposing three, mauve pink to light violet, mid-vein deep pink. Tube slender about as long as the calyx, four stamens.
Habitat: Widespread on calcareous soils and rocks, Pyrenees, France, Alps and Spain, introduced UK.
Family: Scrophulariaceae.

ALPINE TOADFLAX
Linaria alpina

Low, sprawling, hairless annual, biennial or perennial (at high altitudes usually perennial), up to 20cm high. Leaves, sessile, glaucous green, small, linear, oval to narrow-oblong, pointed. Flowers bluish-violet, the lower lip prominence conspicuously marked white or yellow. Spurs long, deeper coloured than the flowers.
Habitat: From 1500m upwards to altitudes of 3,800m, rock faces, screes and light gravel. Throughout the Alps, Apennines and Pyrenees.
Family: Scrophulariaceae.

ANARRHINUM
Anarrhinum bellidifolium

Tall to medium mid-green herb, basal leaves rosetted, oval elliptic, stem leaves deeply contrasting, linear lanceolate borne closely up the stem. Stems branching widely above the middle, leaves much reducing or absent on upper branched stems. Flowers profuse, more or less to one side, small, corolla 5mm long, pale blue to lilac, shortly spurred.
Habitat: Widespread in south-west Europe, in dry areas, fields, rocky hillsides, old walls and hedges.
Family: Scrophulariaceae.

ANDRYALA
Andryala integrifolia

A colourful, fairly distinct, softly hairy annual, to 60cm, conspicuous with its more-or-less flat, bunched display of pale yellow flowers with deeper centre. Outer petals blunt, square-ended. Stems much branched, cream woolly. Leaves all soft hairy, the lower larger slightly toothed and stalked, the upper sessile. Flowers numerous, to 1cm wide, covered below in glandular, pale cream, woolly hairs.
Habitat: Along the Medditeranean to Italy, in dry places, woodland edges, fields, road and track sides.
Family: Compositae.

31.03.09 CONIL

BAELIO
24-04-09 (P)

ANNUAL CONVOLVULUS

Convolvulus tricolor

A dwarf, hairy, spreading annual, easily recognised by its oblong leaves, broader above the centre, narrow to the base, the lower stalked, upper stalkless. Flowers three-coloured, outer circle blue, inner white, throat yellow, large up to 5cm wide, borne on lateral stems, longer than the flowers. Calyx hairy. A pretty annual, cultivated in much-improved and brighter coloured forms for garden display.
Habitat: Widespread in dry sunny places, fields, roadsides, fallow land, light scrub and hedges.
Family: Convolvulaceae.

ANTHEMIS

MIKE'S GARDEN

Anthemis chia

& OUTSIDE OUR HOME - 05-05-09 (P)

Attractively abundant, one of the commonest of the spring camomiles and, like others of this tribe, often paints fields brilliant white in the spring. More-or-less hairless, annual, stem simple branching erect or spreading to 30cm high. Leaves somewhat fern-like, twice pinnate oval oblong in outline, segments broad triangular. Flowers long-stemmed, 3cm across, rayflorets white to 1cm-long disc chrome yellow shorter than the florets. Bracts of flower dark, papery-margined, broad-based, lanceolate, pointed. Aromatic members of this genus are used to make the familiar health beverage, camomile tea.
Habitat: Spain, especially Eastern Mediterranean, Italy and onwards, in dry areas, on fallow and cultivated land, fields, roads and tracksides.
Family: Compositae.

ANTHYLLIS
Anthylis cytisoides

A whip-like erect shrub, up to 80cm, generally recognised by its ball-like or rounded shape and silver-white short-haired stems. Leaves oval elliptic, entire, upper usually divided and trifoliate. Flowers dull yellow, partly hidden by the white-haired calyx, small to 8mm long, borne 3-8 in bract axils. Conspicuous due to its shape, erect whip-like stems and flowers.
Habitat: Native to Spain, France and North Africa, on dry banks, tracks and roadsides, generally within the sea's influence.
Family: Leguminosae.

APHYLLANTHES
Aphyllanthes monspeliensis

Perennial up to 25cm, somewhat unusual for its upright spiky, rush-like appearance. Nevertheless, it frequently makes a handsome bold show when in full flower often appearing as a highly decorative near-gentian blue ball of flowers. Stems tough, ribbed, deep blue-green, leaves tiny, scaly, reduced to red-brown membraneous sheaths. Flowers, wide starry, six petalled, deep blue 25-30mm across with dark central vein, rarely white, terminating two to three on the end of the stems, membraneously sheathed below.
Habitat: Common throughout the Southern Mediterranean, on dry soils, banks and arid areas.
Family: Lilaceae.

N.B. image too pale, colour should be gentian blue.

Seen Oct 08 AFP.

APPLE OF SODOMAEUM

Solanum sodomaeum

Prickly, coarse, untidily branched, hairy perennial shrub, member of the tomato tribe, up to 1m high or more. Leaves deep green oval to broadly triangular, bluntly lobed, veins and leaf stalks prickly spined. Flowers five-petalled to 30mm wide, pale blue, the lower female flowers generally larger than upper male. Stamens conspicuously broadly coned deep yellow. Calyx spined. Fruit a rounded berry, green or yellowish, maturing shiny yellow. More obvious for its yellow fruits, about the size of a cherry tomato than its flowers.

Habitat: Generally near the coast throughout the Mediterranean on waste ground, roadsides and spoil heaps. N.B. Image above natural size.

Family: Solonaceae.

ASPARAGUS

Asparagus acutifolius

A tough, scrambling, woody, pale brown-stemmed perennial up to 1m high sometimes more. Leaves (cladodes) tightly clustered 10-30. small stiff, 3-10mm long by 0.5mm wide, pointed, spiny. Flowers tiny, greenish, six petals, open 3-4mm wide, white star-shaped, two to four thickly clustered within the leaves, closely packed on the stems. Fruits small black. Young shoots often consumed as a popular vegetable.

Habitat: Common throughout the Mediterranean in dry places on light soils, thickets, sands, limestones, garique and the maquis.

Family: Liliaceae.

AUTUMN BUTTERCUP
Ranunculus bullatus

Low, distinct, autumn-flowering buttercup. Flowers solitary on stems ascending to 20cm, usually less, fragrant, bright shining yellow with five to 12 narrowish starry petals more resembling a celandine than a buttercup. Leaves basal, rosetted, light green, round to egg-shaped, toothed, bullate, adpressed to the soil, up to about 8cm across. A pretty, bright, sunny, autumn-flowering plant, providing welcome late colour in October and November.
Habitat: Widespread in Mediterranean region, in light shade on banks, roadsides and rocky areas.
Family: Ranunculaceae.

AUTUMN GRAPE HYACINTH
Muscari parviflorum

Autumn-flowering, low, bulbous, somewhat inconspicuous perennial. Flowers pale blue, sparse, globe-like to bell-shaped, stem sometimes central jointed. Less showy than most other species of Muscari, the only autumn flowering species in the south of Spain.
Habitat: Dry fields, grassland, waste areas, fallow and cultivated land and the garique.
Family: Liliaceae.

BARBARY NUT

Iris sisyrinchium,
Syn: Gynandiris sisyrinchium

Readily distinguished cormed, dwarf iris up to 40cm high, flowers one to four, very sweetly perfumed, pale to deep blue with white centres, yellow-flushed at the base. Leaves few, deep green, narrow grooved and floppy, held near or lying on the ground, usually longer than the flowering stems. A handsome plant, often in colonies when they produce a delightful fragrance. Opening only midday, the flowers remain closed in dull conditions.
Habitat: Common throughout the Mediterranean in dry light soils, on tracksides, footpaths, roadsides and low hills.
Family: Iridaceae.

BERMUDA BUTTERCUP

Oxalis pes-caprae

Winter-flowering bulbous plant, readily recognised for its showy lemon-yellow flowers and shamrock-like, bright green, trefoil leaves, segmented into three broad, heart-shaped leaflets, these downward turning at night and in dull weather. Flowers conspicuous in umbels of six to 12, five-petalled, petals 20-25mm wide. Buds turned downwards. Flowerless in deep shade and on very poor ground. Native of southern Africa introduced late 1800s. Unpalatable to stock and a difficult-to-control agricultural weed. Beautifully colours fields bright gold, December to March.
Habitat: Widespread throughout Mediterranean in fields, olive groves and cultivated land.
Family: Oxalidaceae.

Seen 12-04-08- A.F.P.

BIDENS
Bidens aurea

Autumn-flowering, bearing attractive, bright, yellow-gold, 30-60mm-wide, French marigold-like flowers, often veined purple, central disc prominent, dark brown, yellow or mixed. A tall glabrous perennial, very occasionally up to 1.8cm. Stems branching, soft, easily broken. Leaves thin narrow lanceolate, thinly lobed, fresh green.
Habitat: Naturalised throughout Spain, in damp places. Origin Central America.
Family: Compositae.

BIENNIAL CORNFLOWER
Centaurea pullata

Biennial, usually branched, height variable. Flowers large, terminal in pale shades of pink, rose purple, blue and sometimes white, never brightly coloured. Distinguished by their cornflower-like shape and the conspicuous, wide, green, leafy ruff (involucre) seated immediately below the flower. Involucral bracts, bristly. Leaves angular lobed to triangular, stalked.
Habitat: Widespread at sides of fields, tracks, roads, and in hedges and screes, Spain to France and North Africa.
Family: Comositae.

BINDWEED

Convolvulus arvensis

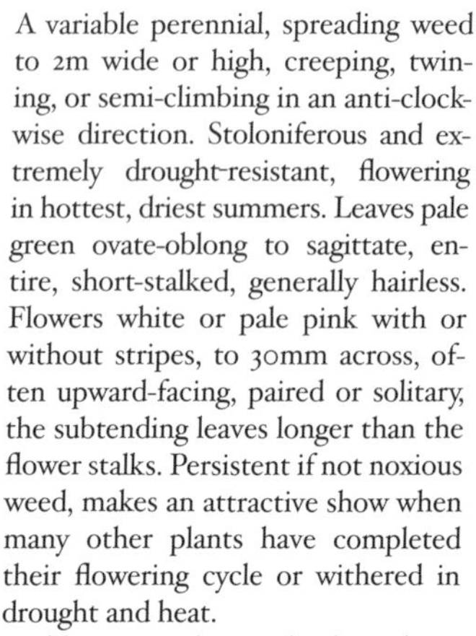

A variable perennial, spreading weed to 2m wide or high, creeping, twining, or semi-climbing in an anti-clockwise direction. Stoloniferous and extremely drought-resistant, flowering in hottest, driest summers. Leaves pale green ovate-oblong to sagittate, entire, short-stalked, generally hairless. Flowers white or pale pink with or without stripes, to 30mm across, often upward-facing, paired or solitary, the subtending leaves longer than the flower stalks. Persistent if not noxious weed, makes an attractive show when many other plants have completed their flowering cycle or withered in drought and heat.

Habitat: Widespread throughout both hemispheres on arable, waste and cultivated land, light turf, railways, gravel, etc.

Family: Convolvulaceae.

BISTORT

Polygonum bistorta

Stout, soft-stemmed perennial, erect, to 1m high, often less. Leaves bright green, triangular lanceolate, longer than wide. The upper sessile, lower with winged stalks. Flowers in dense, pale to bright pink heads, stamens long, protruding. In suitable locations often forms large colonies.

Habitat: Common throughout Europe, ascending to 2,500m in damp fields and meadows, by streams and rivers.

Family: Polygonaceae.

BITTERSWEET, WOODY NIGHTSHADE
Solanum dulcamara

A woody, scrambling or climbing perennial up to 2cm high, immediately recognisable by the distinct shape and colour of its tomato-like flowers. A variable plant, glabrous or tomentose, leaves deep green, entire or strongly lobed. Petiole shorter than the leaves. Flowers in lax cymes, opposite the leaf, downward or outward-facing. Corolla reflexed, blue-purple, rarely white. Berries 1cm wide, attractive, bright shiny green, becoming appealing bright shiny red, egg-shaped. (ovoid).
Habitat: Widespread in temperate regions, including Britain.
Family: Solanaceae.

BLACK NIGHTSHADE
Solanum nigrum

Annual to 60cm pubescent or glabrous stems, usually branched, often darkly coloured purple to blackish. Leaves variable, stalked, dull green, oval-lanceolate margins, shallow-lobed, toothed or entire. Flowers five-petalled small to 14mm across, white usually downward-facing, petals eventually reflexing, anthers yellow, exserted, cone-like to a point, borne three to 10 in wide-branching sprays. Fruit, green berry at first then black, to 8mm wide. Said to be edible raw but contains the alkaloid solanine and some authorities rate it VERY POISONOUS. Cooking or thorough heating can destroy some but not all poisons.
Habitat: Common throughout Europe, the Mediterranean, on waste land, spoil heaps, fallow and cultivated land.
Family: Solanaceae.

BLADDER CAMPION
Silene vulgaris

A greyish, white-flowered, more or less hairless, basal-branching perennial up to 90cm high, at once distinguished by its inflated lantern or balloon-like, purple-netted calyx. Leaves oval lanceolate, basal leaves stalked upwards gradually becoming semi-stem clasping. Flowers 2cm wide borne in loose-spreading terminal racemes. Petals five, white, deeply cut almost to the base. Calyx, expanding in fruit, netted with 20 pale purple veins.
Habitat: Common Europe and the Mediterranean, on track sides, field edges, waste, fallow and cultivated land.
Family: Caryophyllaceae.

BLADDER VETCH
Anthyllis tetraphylla

A low-spreading plant, member of the pea family, immediately recognised by its small pea-like yellow flowers, backed with a larger white standard, quickly followed by bladder-like, clustered, inflated, hairy calyxes, veined light purple. Leaves, pale green, divided into three or five leaflets, the terminal leaflet largest. Flowers 8-12mm long borne laterally, 1-7 in small tight clusters, the whole plant softly hairy.
Habitat: Common Portugal, through southern Spain and North Africa, on dry soils, waste places, the garique, road and track sides, fallow and cultivated fields.
Family: Leguminosae.

BRAMBLE, BLACKBERRY

Rubus sanctus

Readily distinguished by very long, arched, prickly stems, scrambling above the ground or forming near-impenetrable thickets. Leaves green above, divided into three to five, bluish-white below leaflets, the terminal leaflet largest, leaf stems often prickly. Flowers attractive, pink or white, up to 32mm wide, rose-like, stamens often profuse. Fruit succulent, red, ripening to black and shiny. Cultivated, often in thornless forms, for its succulent fruits.

Habitat: Widespread, roadsides, hedgerows, woodlands and rocky banks. In hot areas, the berries shrivel rapidly. Abundant in temperate climates, with more than 80 different species listed in Britain alone.

Family: Rosaceae.

BROAD-LEAVED HELLEBORINE

Epipactis helleborine

Tall, up to 80cm high, rhizomatous, perennial, flowers tending to one side of the stem, stem tip drooping. Lower leaves, four to 10 broad-pointed, upper narrow lanceolate, in spiral arrangement. Flowers widely open, variable in colour, greenish red, or purple to pinkish-green, sepals often with broad green vein. Despite its height tends to be obscure and easily overlooked due to overall grey-green colour.

Habitat: Widespread habitat, light woodlands, sometimes open areas or sand dunes, throughout Mediterranean, native to Britain.

Family: Orchidaceae.

BROOM
Genista sphaerocarpa, syn. Lygos sphaerocarpa

Erect shrub with graceful, spineless, arching branches, up to 2m high or more. Stems cylindrical, much-branched, lightly ribbed. Leaves small lanceolate 0.5cm long, quickly falling away as branches mature. Flowers small, yellow, 12mm long, grouped in small clusters of one to five. Keel hairy, wings pressed back towards the standard. Seed pod, up to 18mm long, calyx hairy.
Habitat: Widespread on dry hills, amid scrub and light trees through the Mediterranean to Italy.
Family: Leguminosae.

BUCKTHORN
Rhamnus oleoides

Deciduous spiny, densely branched shrub to about 1m. Hardly exciting. Stems somewhat rough in texture, grey. Leaves medium-green, small, leathery, linear to oval-linear, short-stalked narrowed to the base, opposite or sometimes in small tight clusters. Flowers tiny, greenish, with or without petals. Fruit rounded, green, later black, soon wrinkling.
Habitat: Spain, local, in scrubby, rocky and sandy areas. A somewhat unappealing shrub forming wide, spiny thickets.
Family: Rhamnaceae.

CHAENORHINUM
Chaenorhinum macrapodum

A fairly vigorous, low, creeping or spreading woolly-haired plant, flowers resembling toadflax, held in small clusters, lilac, with or without a yellow or white throat, the top lip purple-veined. Fruit stalk erect.
Habitat: Dry cliffs and rock faces, southern Spain
Family: Scropulariaceae.

CHRISTMAS IRIS, WIDE-LEAVED IRIS
Iris planifolia

Autumn and winter-growing bulbus perennial. Leaves opposite wide, all basal, shining lustrous green, arching, leek-like. Flowers up to 20cm high, rarely more, delightfully perfumed. Colour deep to light blue or lilac, falls with conspicuous yellow markings, longer than the upright standards.
Habitat: Low-lying, seasonally wet fields, or similar on sloping ground in mountainous areas. Portugal, through southern Spain to North Africa.
Family: Iridaceae.

Seen 29.03.09 - AFP.
" 7.04.09 – Bolote Forest

CISTUS
Cistus crispus

A dark-leaved, low-growing, spreading shrub usually no more than 50cm high. Leaves paired deep green, hairy, three-veined, undulate, stalkless. Flowers a delightful reddish-pink, 3-4cm across, borne in small bunches, but generally not so freely borne as in other Cistus species. Centres, bright yellow bossed, style and stamens of equal length. Sepals five, linear, pointed. C. crispus is possibly the most attractive of the family.
Habitat: Common throughout the Mediterranean area, to North Africa and Italy. In the garique, on dry rocky areas, low hills and woodland edges, preferring acid soils.
Family: Cistaceae.

CLADANTHUS
Cladanthus arabicus

Annual up to 50cm, much resembling single-flowered chrysanthemums, but readily distinguished by its brilliant yellow flowers each surrounded below by a whorl, a ruff of fine fernlike sessile (stemless) leaves. Leaves finely dissected, fern-like.
Habitat: Local in southern Spain, on dry open areas, grassland, fallow and cultivated land. In suitable habitats, forms brilliant eye-catching yellow drifts.
Family: Compositae.

31-03-09 CONIL

CLEMATIS
Clematis flammula

Early to late-flowering perennial, continuing the floral interest and colour well into to the brown shades of Spain's summer landscape. A climber reminiscent of the common well-known wild clematis of northern Spain and the rest of Europe, Old Man's Beard (C. vitalba), but not so vigorous. Leaves two or three times pinnate, leaflets oval oblong leathery greyish green. Flowers four-petalled sometimes five, white 15-30mm across, petal reverse hairy. Borne in conspicuous loose sprays. Stamens wide-spreading. Clumps itself attractively cream-white over low-growing shrubs and tall plants.
Habitat: Common throughout the Mediterranean in dry places, on sand dunes, scrambling and climbing through shrubs and thickets and over dry walls.
Family: Ranunculaceae.

COASTAL CRUCIANELLA
Crucianella maritima

Member of the Bedstraw Family, but hardly the most exciting of plants. Low, sprawling shrub, sometimes prostrate. Branches glabrous, greyish. Leaves thick, leathery, grey-green, close overlapping, margins thinly white, tips spined, borne in crossed fours. Flowers more-or-less insignificant, coralla tubed to 13mm long, twice as long as the bracts and leaves, terminating with five small, dull yellow, inturned lobes. Old dead leaves tend to remain attached to the plant become crisp, dusty, and unsightly.
Habitat: Throughout coastal Spain, in sandy, rocky areas and established sand dunes.
Family: Rubiaceae.

COCKLEBUR
Xanthium strumarium

Fairly readily distinguished coarse annual to about 1cm high, male inflorescence (illustrated). Held in stiff stout spikes of spherical heads vaguely resembling miniature sweet chestnuts to 6mm diameter. Leaves large, long-stalked, triangular-palmate, coarsely toothed, base strongly angular cordate, all slightly rough-haired to the touch. Fruits hairy, hook-spined below to 18mm wide, beaked.
Habitat: Naturalised throughout Europe. Origin possibly North America. In wet places, streams, river sides, marshes, disturbed soils and meadows.
Family: Compositae.

CODLINS AND CREAM
Epilobium hirsutum

Tall to 150cm usually less, softly glandular, hairy, grey-green perennial, often clumping or in numbers growing in close proximity. Leaves sessile, up to 12cm long, mainly opposite, oblong lanceolate with distant incurved teeth, stem-clasping, usually softly hairy both sides. Upper and branch leaves, smaller. Flowers pretty, purple-rose up to 23mm wide, petals short-notched. Stamens attractive, yellow-cream, the inner shorter than outer, the four-lobed stigma exceeding the stamens.
Habitat: Widespread Spain, rest of Europe, in moist places near rivers, streams, water channels, canals and ditches.
Family: Onagraceae.

COLUMBINE
Aquilegia vulgaris

A pretty flowering perennial herb up to 1m high, usually less, branching above. Stems with or without hairs, blackish towards the base. Leaves glaucous green, glabrous basal, long-stalked three-lobed, irregular, upper shorter ascending into bracts. Flowers large nodding, 3-5cm across in irregular cymes, overall deepish blue, sometimes white or deep pink, spur slightly longer than the 30mm-long petals, ending abruptly incurved, with knobbed tips. Fruits five-carpelled. Widely cultivated for its dainty flowers and hybridised into many-coloured, long, short-spurred varieties.
Habitat: Widespread throughout the northern hemisphere, across Europe and Asia in damp places on calcareous soils, in light shade.
Family: Ranunculaceae.

COMFREY
Symphytum officinale

Soft green perennial to 120cm, leaves large, oval lanceolate, the lower stemmed. Upper smaller, winged downwards and softly long-haired. Stem hairs long deflexed, stems branching near the top, branches decurrent to the stem. Flowers pendant, in small groups, tubed. Corolla in shades of white to cream pink or purplish, up to 17mm long. Calyx 7-8mm long, teeth exceeding tube. Leaves once used as a poultice.
Habitat: Europe, central Spain northwards, in damp places near streams and rivers.
Family: Boraginaceae.

COMMON AGRIMONY

Agrimonia eupatoria

Perennial, tall, erect up to 60cm, usually single-stemmed. Leaves, fresh green, greyish below three to six-pinnate, the lower smaller than the upper, edges coarsely toothed. Flowers at right angles to the stem, small, 5-8cm wide, chrome yellow. Fruits grooved and spiny. Conspicuous when in flower, but not showy.
Habitat: Widespread. Prefers shady places, hedgerows, woodland edges, roadsides, field edges.
Family: Rosaceae.

COMMON CENTAURY

Centaurium erythraea, Syn C. majus

A short to medium-height biennial, usually single-stemmed, branching above into a broad array of attractive flowers, in a distinct shade of pink. Basal leaves rosetted, strongly three to five-veined. Tending to die away as the plant commences flowering.
Habitat: Common throughout Europe in dry places, in light grassland. open scrubland and open woodland, usually on calcareous soils.
Family: Gentianaceae.

29.03.09 - AFP.
Sun 12.04.08 - Vejer

COMMON BORAGE

Borago officinalis

Stout, hispid, annual herb 30–60cm high. Easily recognised by its conspicuous leafy, spreading axillary and terminal cymes of well-spaced blue, downward to outward-facing star-shaped, white, centred flowers, with purple-black protruding stamens. Flower stalks sometimes attractively reddish in colour. The whole plant hairy, leaves large 10-20cm, ovate to oblong, bluntly toothed, gradually becoming smaller and stem-clasping higher up the stem. Long cultivated as a herb, now on wider scale for its rich, oil-producing seeds.

Habitat: Widespread along Mediterranean, favouring waste and cultivated land near habitation.

Family: Boraginaceae.

COMMON COW WHEAT

Melampyrum pratense

Branched variable annual, up to 50cm high. Readily distinguished by its pale to bright yellow, two-lipped flowers, 12-22mm long. Interior bright yellow, loosely held in a lax spike, flowers turned to one side of the stem. Leaves linear lanceolate, opposite, short-stalked, strongly mid veined.

Habitat: Widespread throughout Europe, including central Spain, Portugal, in woodlands, fileds tracksides and hedges. A semi-parasite.

Family: Scropulariaceae.

31-03 09 CONIL

Seen 12-04-08 AFP

COMMON MALLOW

Malva sylvestris

A variable, robust, sometimes untidy-looking biennial or perennial to 1.5m, stems erect or decumbent, sparsely hairy. Basal leaves long-stalked, roundish, base cordate, shallowly lobed and lightly folded. Stem leaves deeply five to seven crenately lobed and lightly hairy. Flowers clustered two or more on axillary stalks, raceme-like, rose pink to light purple, conspicuously dark-purple-veined. Petals, not over-lapping, up to 30cm long, two to four times longer than the calyx. Calyx lobes ovate-triangular, connivent, constant in the fruiting stage.

Habitat: Common throughout Europe on dry soils, waste places, roadsides, banks, fallow and cultivated land.

Family: Malvaceae.

COMMON MILKWORT

Polygala serpyllifolia

Low slender-stemmed, the lower stems slightly woody, and the lower leaves smaller than upper, opposite, ovate. Upper elliptic to lanceolate. Inflorescence three to eight flowered, short to dense. Flowers bright, gentian blue, or slate-blue. Inner sepals longer and broader than capsule, veins branched to form loops.

Habitat: Widespread in Europe, including the Pyrenees and Britain, in grassy areas and limy soils.

Family: Polygalaceae.

ARCOS - 08·04·09

COMMON MORNING GLORY
Ipomea purpurea

A vigorous, handsome, profusely flowered perennial, bearing distinct large purple flowers. A left-twisting climber, festooning itself, through or over, trees, hedges, fences, scrub and dry banks in wafts of purple. Leaves large, up to 14cm long by 13cm wide, very variable, greyish green, heart-shaped to triangular cordate with or without bluntly pointed, long, acuminate, opposing lobes. Stems and leaves, light, bristly, hairy. Flowers large, trumpet-shaped, up to 8cm across and 6cm long, deep royal purple merging to deep rose centres. Calyx with five short linear, pointed teeth, almost one-third the length of the tube.

Habitat: A sun-loving garden escape of South American origin, frequent in coastal regions, cultivated or escaped. Long flowering.

Family: Convolvulaceae.

COMMON POPPY, FIELD POPPY
Papaver rhoeas

ZAHARA PALACETE 29·04·09 (P)

A variable annual, 30-60cm tall, erect, bristly. Leaves, dark green, basal leaves stalked, twice-pinnate, upper stalkless (sessile), singly pinnate, the central lobe extended. Flowers 7-10cm across, scarlet to crimson, occasionally pink or white, petals broadly rounded, with or without a blue-black basal blotch. Seed capsule twice as long as wide. White latex exuding on broken or damaged stems. Beautiful flower, romantically associated with paintings, perfumes and war (the poppies of Flanders fields). A parent of the cultivated annual Shirley poppies.

Habitat: Widespread, in disturbed soils, cultivated fields and roadsides.

Family: Papaveraceae.

COMMON SMILAX

Smilax aspera

A shrubby, tough, scrambling or climbing plant, leaves generally heart-shaped, with paired tendrils at the base. Dark green, often marbled white, usually margined with evenly spaced sharp prickles. Male and female flowers (male illustrated), borne on separate plants. Fruits, small red globular berries. The young edible shoots can be consumed like cultivated asparagus.

Habitat: Widespread, in hedgerows, the garique and dry places.

Family: Liliaceae.

COMMON TOADFLAX

Linaria vulgaris

Hairless perennial up to 80cm high. Usually many-stemmed, erect, branching above, stoloniferous below. Leaves narrow, linear lanceolate, sometimes broad linear up to 8cm long. Flowers up to 20, closely borne on long racemes, long-spurred, spur straight, whitish, almost as long as the corolla. Corolla pale yellow, up to 25cm long, centre prominence, bright orange.

Habitat: Common through Europe but rare in southern Spain. On waste land, in grass, by hedges, on banks, in cultivated and fallow fields.

Family: Scrophulariaceae.

COMMON VINE, GRAPE

Vitis vinifera

Well-known plant cultivated for its succulent fruits, often escaping to the wild or living on in abandoned cultivations. Vigorous, scrambling or climbing stems to 35m, long, flexible, tough, roughly angular. Leaves large, palmate, coarsely toothed, five to seven-lobed, usually individually offset by an opposing tendril. Flowers tiny, profuse, cream or greenish in large panicles, strongly pulled downwards as the fruits develop weight. Fruit ripening to various colours, from whitish-green to red, or purple-black, often with bloom, oval, juicy.
Habitat: Long cultivated throughout the Mediterranean and elsewhere.
Family: Vitaceae.

CORN SALAD

Valeriana echinata

A slightly hairy, thickish, stemmed little-branched, pale green annual up to 20cm high. Flowers pink, held in small terminal, usually twice-divided heads. Calyx diagnostic with two short lobes and one long lobe. Fruits reminiscent of small knobkerries, three clustered with curved spines, one larger and longer than the other two.
Habitat: Common throughout the Mediterranean and Morocco in light shade, hedgerows, rocky areas near fields and thickets. Gregarious, often colonising small areas in colourful pink drifts.
Family: Valerianeacea.

CORSICAN HEATH

Erica terminalis

Low, upright evergreen shrub up to 1m high, branches sub-erect, minutely haired. Leaves small linear, 4-6mm in whorls of four, hairless (glabrous) held at right angles to the stem. Flowers bright rose-pink, ovoid bell-shaped, to 7mm long, borne in terminal clusters of three to eight. Stamens not protruding.

Habitat: Southwest Spain, southern Italy and islands. In damp sandy places, streamsides, light woodland and the maquis, on acid soils.

Family: Ericaceae.

CREEPING GROMWELL

Lithospermum diffusum

Attractive flowering, spreading to semi-erect, hairy, perennial sub-shrub, to 80cm high, often less. Leaves alternate, narrow deep green to 2cm long, hairy above, pale below, outer edges deeply inrolled. Flowers an appealing bright deep blue, corolla to 2cm long, wide opening at the mouth into five round lobes, calyx hairy. Prized and cultivated in the UK for the colour of its flowers.

Habitat: Widespread Spain to southern France in shrubby places, scrambling among vegetation, in light woodland and rocky places.

Family: Boraginaceae.

CROCUS

Crocus serotinus, Ssp. salzmannii (see also Saffron crocus)

Low-growing, large-cormed autumn flowering perennial. Leaves dark green, erect, thinly narrow, 3-5mm wide, usually only part showing at the flowering stage. Flowers appealing, shiny purple to lilac, often lightly veined and yellow-throated. Tepals (petals) up to 50mm long, pointed, wider above the centre, generally bluntish. Croci are distinguished from Colchicums by having three, rather than six, stamens.
Habitat: Rocky and sandy areas, open pine woodland, sparse grassland.
Family: Iridaceae.

CROSSWORT

Cruciata laevipes

Scrambling and creeping square-stemmed basal branching perennial, leaves in crossed fours, 12 to 20mm oval to elliptic pale yellow-green, strongly veined. Flowers, tiny bright yellow, numerous, borne in whorls in the axils of the leaves, four petals squared to form a cross. Strongly honey scented. Fruits small black. The whole, soft hairy to the touch. Straggly, yellowish plant, heavy fragrance.
Habitat: Widespread throughout Europe, absent from the eastern Mediterranean, in hedges, pastures, waysides and open fields, generally on calcareous soils.
Family: Rubiaceae.

Seen 12.04.08 AGP

CROWN DAISY

Chrysanthemum coronarium, Syn. Dendranthema coronarium

A strongly vigorous and showy, readily recognised, much-branched annual up to 90cm, bearing large, conspicuous, white, daisy-like 5cm-wide flowers, broadly orange circled at the centre or sometimes all lemon yellow. Involucral bracts, outer ovoid brown banded. Inner pale with small appendage and dry wide margins. Leaves bright green, stalkless, cut into fern-like linear segments. The familiar generic name Chrysanthemum has been botanically discarded in favour of Dendranthema.

Habitat: Portugal and throughout the Mediterranean, on light soils, waste land, roads, track sides and disturbed ground.

Family: Compositae.

CRYPTOSTEMMA

Cryptostemma calendula

Low-stature perennial. Leaves irregular, cut into rounded-end lobes, the terminal lobe triangular, bigger than the two to four pairs of lateral lobes, pale to dull green above, greyish-white tomentose below, formed into a very lax rosette. Flowers calendula-like up to 4cm wide, long-stalked, solitary, rays yellow with deeper central ring. Disc black, yellowed with stamens. Fruit hairy.

Habitat: Native of South Africa but strongly naturalised along the coast of Portugal and Spain on light soils and sand.

Family: Compositae.

CUPIDONE

Catanache caerulea

Medium to tall, thin-stemmed plant bearing solitary, large, broad-petalled, singularly beautiful, pale blue, violet-centred flowers. Florets blunt-ended, five-toothed, strongly parallel veined. Stigmas protruding, long filamentous. Involucral bracts papery silver, central vein brown. Much cultivated for the beauty of its flowers.
Habitat: Widespread, central and southern Spain, France, on roadsides, in dry meadows, bushy places and the garique.
Family: Compositae.

CURRY PLANT

Helichrysum stoechas

Low, strongly aromatic shrub, smelling strongly of curry if bruised or gathered. Stems grey to whitish, strong, wiry, erect up to 75cm high, terminating in flattish close corymbs of 10-35. The chrome yellow flowers are enveloped and partly hidden in shiny membraneous yellowish bracts. Sometimes, to secondary flower heads arise on the same stem. Leaves small, revolute, untoothed white-felted.
Habitat: Common throughout Europe in dry areas, sandy rocky places in highlands and lowlands.
Family: Compositae.

CUT-LEAVED LAVENDER
Lavandula multifida

Possibly the least attractive of the lavenders. Growth lax, untidy, usually up to about 50cm high, of an overall grey-green colour. Flower heads small, carried on long leafless stalks, few on the heads. Usually not more than three flowers at one time, individual flowers up to 1.5cm long. Leaves toothed, twice pinnate. To some find its smell strong and unpleasant.
Habitat: Dry hills, roadsides, rocky areas on arid soils, common through Portugal and the Mediterranean.
Family: Labiateae

CYTINUS
Cytinus hypocistis

An odd, totally parasitic plant living on the roots of Cistus species. Its flowers appear in small clumps just above soil level, without leaves, near or below the host plant. Flower colour variable, according to the sub-species and the Cistus host. The most colourful have carmine bracts, centred by yellow flowers. Flowers fleshy, about 15 in clusters, 4-8cm high. Corolla bell-shaped, four-petalled, male flowers above, female below.
Habitat: Widespread in the Mediterranean area, has to be searched for, at the edges of thin woodland, the garrigue and maquis.
Family: Rafflesiaceae.

12 04 09 AFP (P)

DAPHNE
Daphne gnidium

An upright, somewhat leggy, evergreen shrub to 120cm, leaves pale green, thickish, narrow lanceolate to 4cm long, usually becoming terminal on flowering stems, young branches softly brown haired. Flowers, slightly fragrant, tubed, exterior hairy, small, white to pale cream, reflexing at the end to form four small, broadly triangular "petals". Fruits, bright red to black ovoid berries. Poisonous, has purgative properties.
Habitat: Common in Portugal, south-west Spain, Greece, Turkey and North Africa. In dry areas, among light shrub, thin woodland, on hillsides, low mountains, and the garique.
Family: Thymelaeaceae.

DIPCADI
Dipcadi serotinum

An unusually coloured, low to medium, bulbous plant. Distinguished by its pendant, bluebell-like flowers, arranged to one side of the stem, in an indistinguishable shade of khaki-green. Can be dificult to spot.
Habitat: Widespread in Spain, on dry sandy soils, rocky places, among light grass and shrubs.
Family: Liliaceae.

POSSIBLE SPOTTING BYG ?
27-03-09 AFP

DORYCNIUM

Dorycnium hirsuta

Hairy perennial, somewhat spreading, up to 50cm high, woody at the base. Leaves barely stalked, divided into three leaflets accompanied by two similar leaflike stipules, all softly hairy with hairy margins. Flowers to 6mm long, standard white flushed pink, keel conspicuous deep purple borne in dense white, woolly, terminal, leaf-fringed corymbs. Calyx profusely white-haired. Fairly easily recognised by its wide, white, cottony, hairy flower-heads and subtending green-fringed corymbs.

Habitat: Common throughout Spain and Europe in dry places, on field edges, track-sides, banks, sandy and rocky places.

Family: Leguminosae.

DROSOPHYLLUM

Drosophyllum lusitanicum

Perennial herb up to 30cm high, stems upright solitary or branched. Leaves before flowering rosetted, later less crowded and moving up the stem, lower leaves sometimes dying during flowering, long, narrow, gradually tapering to a point, red gland tipped on the surface and sides. Flowers pale yellow up to 40cm across, five-petalled, glandular on the upper stem and calyx. The only insectiverous plant in southern Spain. To overcome the lack of essential salts, especially nitrates, in acid soils, the plant traps small insects on its sticky glands, gradually digesting their soft body parts.

Habitat: On coasts or near coastal areas southern Spain and Portugal, on dry acid soils, in the garique and maquis. Has to be searched for.

Family: Droseraceae (Sundews).

DUTCHMAN'S PIPE

Aristolochia baetica

Perennial, tough, glabrous, evergreen climber, up to 3m in height, sometimes sprawling, leaves stalked, rather dull grey-green, leathery, up to 5cm long, heart-shaped. Flowers, unmistakable, velvet dark-maroon, to 7cm long, tubed, strongly U-curved to open at the mouth, fat, wide, prominent at the base of the curved tube. Long-flowering, January to July. Known to have been used as an antidote for snake bites, and against fevers and for abortion purposes.

Habitat: Portugal through to south-east Spain and North Africa, usually in semi-shade, climbing from the base of trees, shrubs and thickets in fairly low altitudes.

Family: Aristolochiaceae.

DWARF ELDER, DANEWORT

Sambucus ebulus

A tall, very upright perennial to 2m high, bearing large, flat umbels of purple anthered white, or sometimes pink flowers. Leaves, large pinnate, leaflets five to 13, deep green, ovate oblong, sharply serrate. Umbels flat, densely flowered up to16mm wide. Berries round, green, ripening to blackish-purple. Leaves smell of elderberry.

Habitat: Widespread, central and southern Europe, also the UK, on damp soils. Near ditches, streams, waste places, light scrub and roadsides.

Family: Caprifoliaceae.

ELDERBERRY
Sambucus nigra

Well-known, small-to-medium deciduous shrub bearing wide, flat heads (panicles) of pearly white to cream flowers, followed by black berries with reddish stems. Leaves, pinnate, yellowish, the whole plant with the distinctive smell of elderberry. The berries are used to make wine, but the flowers provide a superior product. Hay fever sufferers beware — gathering the flowers can provoke severe hay fever attacks.
Habitat: Widespread on dryish soils, common in the UK.
Family: Caprifoliaceae.

ENGLISH LAVENDER
Lavendula angustifolia

A familiar, low, shrubby, strongly aromatic plant, common to English gardens, bearing spikes of highly perfumed pale lavender-coloured flowers, terminating the long leafless stems. The grey-green narrow linear leaves are copiously borne, well below the flowers. Much used in preparation of perfumes and oils. Lavender farms are a tourist attraction in Britain and France where white, pink, blue and deep purple flowered forms may be observed. Unfortunately, highly coloured varieties often lack fragrance.
Habitat: Common throughout Europe on dry banks, stony areas, the garique and roadsides. Widely cultivated both ornamentally and commercially.
Family: Labiatae.

ETRUSCAN HONEYSUCKLE

Lonicera etrusca

Deciduous, climber or scrambler up to 4m high. Leaves pale, bluish to whitish green, ovate oblong to 8cm long, the lower with or without short stalks, upper fused together ringing the stem. Flowers long, narrow, thinly trumpet-shaped, up to 4cm long in clusters up to 20 or more, the clusters borne in threes, often with lesser flowered lower clusters. Exteriors deep cream, with or without red or purple flushes, slightly fragrant. Fruits red, small egg-shaped.

Habitat: Widespread in copses, woodlands and scrub thoughout southern Europe on limestone soils.

Family: Caprifoliaceae.

EVENING PRIMROSE

Oenothera biennis

Biennial plant of European and British gardens, native to North America and naturalised throughout central Europe. Usually a strong to vigorous plant, up to 1m high, easily distinguished by its attractive evening opening, scented, large, golden-yellow flowers with equal length, stamens and stigmas. Leaves, soft green short-stalked, often reddish on mature plants, oblong lanceolate, centre vein strong, whitish. A handsome, flowering, old-fashioned garden plant, its therapeutic qualities utilised in essential oil products.

Habitat: Roadside verges, field edges, and banks.

Family: Onagraceae.

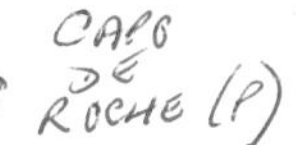

EVERGREEN CANDYTUFT

Iberis sempervirens

Low, shrubby, hairless, much-branched, wiry-stemmed, dark-leaved spreading ever-green up to 25cm high. Leaves small, narrow, thick spatula-shaped, dark green above, paler beneath up to 3.5cm long. Flowers white, four-petalled in flat-topped heads borne on lateral shoots, lengthening in fruit. Fruits: siliculas, deeply notched and winged to 7mm long.

Habitat: West to central Mediterranean, in rocky areas of high hills and mountains. A surprisingly tough plant frequently used as border edging in the UK.

Family: Crucifereae.

EVERLASTING PEA

Lathyrus latifolius

A colourful perennial, immediately recognisable as a colourful member of the pea tribe. Stems variable, broad to narrow-winged. Flowers large, to 30cm wide, sweet pea-like, borne up to 10 on long leafless stems. Standard bright pink, keel a little paler. Leaves tendrilled, in narrow pairs, with or without hairs, glaucous, veins five, parallel. A bright, attractive, very visible plant, frequently cultivated. Scentless, as distinct from the highly fragrant annual sweet pea.

Habitat: Widespread through the Mediterranean, climbing, sprawling or clambering on tracks, hillsides, through plants and shrubs in dry areas.

Family: Leguminosae.

FEDIA
Fedia cornucopiae

Medium to low, pale green, somewhat soft fleshy annual, often spring colouring fields purple. Leaves opposite, lower spatula-shaped upper stalkless, broadly toothed and strongly veined. Corolla two-lipped, 8 -16mm long, light purple, stamens prominent, flowers held in tight clusters above the leaves. Calyx conspicuous, bronze red.
Habitat: Widespread, west to central Mediterranean in waste places, fields, cultivated and fallow land, tracksides, banks and rocky areas.
Family: Valerianaceae.

FELTY GERMANDER
Teucrium polium

A very variable, low-spreading, whitish or grey felted sub-shrub, up to 45cm high. Flowers in dense round to more-or-less conical heads, cream-white to pinkish. Corolla slightly longer than the calyx, stamens not projecting. Leaves small, stalkless, generally oblong to ovate, toothed with smooth inrolled margins. Stems, with white to pale gold, cotton-like hairs, upright and woody. Has medicinal uses, for fevers, colds and stomach problems.
Habitat: Widespread throughout the Mediterranean, generally near coasts in light arid soils, screes, sand, rocky areas, and light woodland .
Family: Labiatae.

FIELD DODDER

Cuscuta campestris

The three species of dodder native to Spain are extremely difficult to separate and identify. C. campestris, illustrated, is native to North America and has white to pink, five partate flowers and yellow stems. The life history of the dodders is precarious. Germinating seedlings give rise to a long slender shoot attached to a very weak root. The stem describes a circular motion searching for a suitable host plant on which to attach itself. If it fails, it dies. If successful, it feeds on its host, its own root quickly dying away.
Habitat: Widespread, but very local and has to be searched for.
Family: Convolvulaceae.

FIELD MARIGOLD

Calendula arvensis

Bright, small-flowered annual, flowers 1 to 2cm across, solitary, in shades of orange to yellow, the central disc similar or in slightly darker shades. Habit spreading to erect to 30cm high, branches thinly hairy. Leaves, oblong lanceolate, faintly toothed or untoothed. Fruits diagnostic, held in three rows, the outer row of achenes slender, sickle-shaped, with spiny exterior. The centre row, broad, boat-shaped and the inner row curved into a ring. Long-flowering, from November to March or April.
Habitat: Common in fields, fallow, waste ground and roadsides, often colouring whole areas in sheets of pale orange yellow.
Family: Compositae

Seen 06.04.08
AFP

FORGET-ME-NOT TREE
Wigandia caracasana

A rather coarse, broad-leaved, evergreen, wide-spreading shrub, up to 5m high. Distinguished by its deep blue racemes of forget-me-not-like flowers. Leaves large, prominently mid-veined, scabrid to the touch, margins crenate, dark green above, paler below. Flowers many in loose racemes, up to 1cm wide, petals five, broad, overlapping, rounded, centres marked white. Stamens protruding, conspicuous. In flower, highly visible and attractive. A garden escape.
Habitat: Not native to Spain but appears to be increasing on the Mediterranean coast on wasteland and roadsides.
Family: Boraginaceae.

FOXGLOVE
Digitalis purpurea

Readily distinguished by purple-pink, finger-glove-like pendant flowers, the lower protruding, pale-tipped lower lip and black, purple-spotted interior with white surround. Tall biennial, 50 -150cm stem, simple or branched. Leaves rosetted, ground-hugging, large, to 30cm long, green, distinctly crenate, softly hairy above, tomentose below, tending to die away as the flower spike develops and smaller new leaves ascend the stem. Flowers nodding 20 to 80, raceme one-sided. Poisonous, a source of the important medicinal drug, digitalin.
Habitat: Common throughout cool acid woods, heaths and rocky areas. Common in UK woodlands, occurs in woodlands of southwest Spain. Cultivated in improved garden forms.
Family: Scrophulariaceae.

FRAGRANT BUG ORCHID

Orchis coriophora, Ssp. fragrans

A rather inconspicuous orchid, flowers an overall dusky pink shade. An erect slender plant up to 40cm high, usually less. Leaves long, narrow, pointed, generally upright. Flowers lax or densely held 10-12mm long, on upright spikes. Hood pointed, brownish-purple, streaked green. Lip wine-purple, becoming paler and green towards the centre, three-lobed, the two side lobes shorter than the centre lobe. Stem bracts 1cm long decreasing in length up the stem. Reputedly smells of bed bugs, while the fragrans sub species is lightly vanilla-scented.
Habitat: Common throughout the Mediterranean, in grassland and among light shrubs, in damp or dry areas.
Family: Orchidaceae.

FRENCH LAVENDER

Lavendula stoechas

Easily identifed by its large, attractive, bright purple bracts distinctly ornamenting the flower heads. A greyish green, softly hairy pleasantly aromatic linear-leaved shrub, rarely up to1m high. Leaves entire with thick edges. Flowers profuse. Very small 6-8mm, held in squat, squarish spikes, at once conspicuous due to the large oblong 10-50mm long purple, rarely white bracts, topping the spike. Quite colourful when viewed grouped and flowering in small colonies.
Habitat: Widespread, dry rocky places, light scrub and woodland, roadsides and the garique. Garden-cultivated for ornament, commercially for perfume.
Family: Labiateae

Seen 06.04.08 AFP
29.03.09-AFP

FRINGED PINK
Dianthus monspessulanus

Perennial up to 60cm, stems slender, leaves and stems glaucous. Readily distinguished by its large pale pink or whitish, lightly fragrant flowers, the petals deeply lacinated to form a conspicuous fringe, the uncut portion wider than the cut lobes or fringes. This plant may be a parent of colourful British garden hybrids marketed under the name Sweet Wiversfield.

Habitat: Meadows, sandy places, woodland fringes, Portugal, Spain to the Alps.

Family: Caryophyllaceae.

FRINGED RUE
Ruta chalepensis

Readily recognised by its overall yellow-green colour, including petal fringes, and fetid smell. A lax-branched perennial, woody below, up to 70cm high. Leaves glaucous, foetid, twice pinnate, lobes oblong wedge-shaped. Flowers yellow-green, petals with upstanding fringes.

Habitat: A widespread plant in the Mediterranean, on dry areas, banks, tracksides, scrub edges, thickets and sandy places.

Family: Rutaceae, of which all the citrus fruits are also members.

GENISTA

Genista equisetiformis

Low, dense, evergreen shrub, to 60cm tall, stems ribbed, rush-like, with thin lateral branches. Leaves alternate, silvery, tiny scale-like, to 2mm long. Flower heads spherical irregular, star-shaped, stem-terminating, with up to 20 flowers a head. Flowers bright yellow to 1.5cm long. Calyx and petals densely hairy, bracts leaf-like. Standard and keel, of more or less equal length.
Habitat: Spain, banks, rocky places, road and track sides in hot dry areas.
Family: Leguminosae.

GENISTA

Genista hirsuta

Lowish spiny shrub, flowers yellow in bright pyramidal spikes. Lateral branches small, much crowded, ends sharply spiny, immature branches hairy. Leaves small lanceolate up to 1cm long. Flowers in sharply cone-shaped spikes, the long silky hairs on both the calyx and petals, diagnostic, all crowded, terminating the ends of the lateral branches. Individual flowers up to 1.25mm long, standards less, to half the size of the keel.
Habitat: Common Portugal, western Spain, Morocco on light sandy soils, low hills and mountains, on rocky banks and scrub.
Family: Leguminosae.

12·04·09 AFP (P)

GERMANDER SPEEDWELL
Veronica chamaedrys

Prostrate perennial herb, nodal rooting, stems becoming erect and bearing two lines of white hairs on opposite sides of the stem. Leaves medium-green, 2.3cm long, opposite oval-pointed, margins round-toothed, sub-sessile. Flowers bright pale blue, up to 6mm wide, white-throated, borne in long, pyramidal racemes. Bracts linear, calyx lanceolate.
Habitat: Common to dry soils, short grassland, hedgerows, woodsides and heaths throughout Europe, Portugal, central and northern Spain.
Family: Scrophulariaceae.

GIANT FENNEL
Ferula communis

A giant of a plant, sometimes up to 5m high, readily recognisable due to its great size and huge ferny leaves, which die away after flowering, and green-yellow flowered umbels. Stem hollow, solitary or branched, thick, stout. Leaves deep green, soft, split into many thread-like four-pinnate segments. Lower cylindrically stalked, upper with large sheathing bases.
Habitat: Common throughout the Mediterranean, in calcareous soils in dry areas, on roadsides, hills, waste ground.
Family: Umbelliferae.

GIANT ORCHID
Barlia robertiana

Stout reddish-stemmed perennial up to 60cm high. Leaves large, broadly oval lanceolate, forming a loose basal rosette, stem leaves few, smaller, oval lanceolate. Flowers dense, in long, broad, heavy spikes, wine-purple. Hood wide, purple green, forward-pointing. Labellum long with two rather wide, strap-shaped, arm-like lobes. Basal lobes broad, widely divided, leg-like.
Habitat: Common throughout the Mediterranean, on stony, grassy banks, the maquis and the garique.
Family: Orchidaceae.

GIANT REED CANE
Arunda donax

Readily recognised, giant bamboo-like grass up to 5m high, the largest in Europe. Thought to have originated in the Orient, cultivated and naturalised in Spain for many years. Stems thick, woody, usually in broad dense thickets, stems shiny bamboo-like when dry polished and devoid of leaves. Leaves large, long 2.5cm wide, hairy-liguled at the base. Flowers in large, wide-spreading, light-coloured plumes (darkening later), to 70cm deep. Old plumes narrowing and becoming pale brown.
Habitat: Common throughout the Mediterranean in damp places, often near the coast. Widely used to form windbreaks, plant supports, etc.
Family: Graminae.

21.04.09 - CAPO DE ROCHE (P)

GIANT THAPSIA

Thapsia garganica

Attractive plant, up to 2m high, sometimes more. Stems solid, erect, smooth or grooved. Leaves large, two to three-pinnate (fern-like), pale below, green above, segments oblong, narrow. Gradually reducing up the stem to broad, inflated, basal sheathes. Flowers, rayed up to 25, carried in large globular umbels, bright yellow-green, bractless. Fruits, seeds with two papery, silvery-brown wings to each edge. Picturesquely lights up wide areas golden yellow-green.

Habitat: Widespread, Portugal through the Mediterranean, in rocky areas, at woodland edges, in dry places, preferring limestone soils.

Family: Umbelliferae.

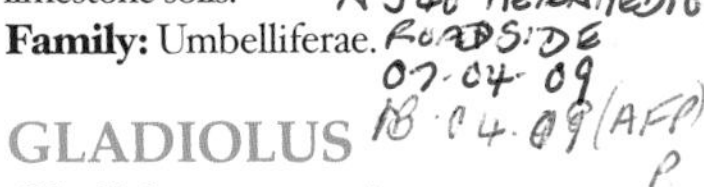

GLADIOLUS

Gladiolus communis

The colourful flower spikes of the cormed genus Gladioli may be readily recognised. Separating the species is more difficult. G. communis is rather similar to the deep-pink-flowered G. segetum, but differs in that its flowers are generally held to one side of the stem. Bracts, less than the length of the flower above, petals of equal size, except the upper central, which is slightly larger. Stamens equal to, or shorter than, the filaments.

Habitat: Dry areas throughout the Mediterranean, in woodland, scrub edges, banks, fields and waste ground, naturalised in the UK.

Family: Iridaceae.

Seen 6-04-08
A.F.P
29-03-09
AFP

GLOBE THISTLE

Echinops ritro

Perennial, tall to medium height, thistle-like, bearing attractive, steel-blue globular heads of flowers up to 45mm across, borne on strong erect stems. Leaves usually white-felted below, once or twice pinnate, tipped with slender spines. Margins curving downwards.
Habitat: Widespread in dry areas, on grassy banks, roadsides, stony fields and pastures.
Family: Compositae.

GOLDEN DOG'S TAIL GRASS

Lamarckia aurea

A tufted grass to about 15cm high, leaves thin, linear to 1mm across, edges rough and similarly so on the stems below the inflorescence, up to 10mm long, ligules membraneous. Glumes 3-4mm long. Lemma stiffly awned to 12mm across. Distinguished by its attractive, green-gold, one-sided, plume-like inflorescence, in the form of a well-groomed dog's tail.
Habitat: Widespread throughout Europe on dry soils, waste places, roadsides.
Family: Gramineae.

GRASS-LEAVED BUTTERCUP

Ranunculus gramineus

Upright or somewhat sprawling perennial, distinguished by its smooth, grass-like glaucous stems and stemless leaves. Flowers solitary, individually showy, large golden-yellow, 2-3cm wide, opening almost flat.
Habitat: Southern Spain, in dry open and rocky areas.
Family: Ranunculaceae.

GRAPE HYACINTH

Muscari neglectum

Attractive, bulbous perennial, immediately recognised by its heads of deep blue bell-shaped flowers up to 7mm long, with tiny, narrowly tipped white teeth. Heads carried stiffly on short stalks, flowers 10 to 15 in small dense racemes. Upper flowers sterile, light blue tending to be outward or upward-facing. Leaves all basal, bright green, cylindrical, channelled, narrowly linear lanceolate.
Habitat: Widespread, throughout the Mediterranean, in fields, hills, rocky areas, fallow and cultivated land and vineyards. Species and hybrids of this genus commonly ornament British gardens.
Family: Liliaceae.

GREAT REEDMACE, BULLRUSH

Typha latifolia

A robust perennial, so well known as to require little description. Leaves up to seven upright, linear, 18-22mm across, tall, reaching higher than the inflorescence. Flowers unisexual, male above, female below. The similar, less common lesser reedmace (T. angustifolia) has narrower leaves, up to 10mm wide.

Habitat: Widespread throughout Europe in silting and silted-up rivers, canals, ponds, lakes and marshes, often the dominant plant.

Family: Typhaceae.

GREATER CELANDINE

Chelidonium majus

A member of the poppy family, this bears no resemblance to the lesser celandine (of the buttercup family), apart from the colour of its flowers. A soft-stemmed, tall perennial, up to 90cm high, at once distinguished by its four-petalled flowers and prominent yellow stamens, plus the unusual shape of the hairy flower buds. Leaves, green, soft hairy, alternately pinnate with large round-toothed, lobes, sometimes decurrent, with or without short-stalked hairy stems.

Habitat: Widespread in temperate areas on grassy banks, old walls and hedgerows.

Family: Paperavacea.

GREEN STONECROP
Sedum sediforme

Perennial with conspicuous succulent, swollen, pointed glaucous leaves distinguished when in flower by the curiously arranged outward-spreading, branched flower heads arranged rather like the spokes of an umbrella, stiffly held on more-or-less, non-leafy stems 30 to 50cm high. Non-flowering stems very leafy. Flowers petalled yellow-green, five to eight, outward-spreading.
Habitat: Common throughout Europe and the Mediterranean on calcareous rocky hills and mountains up to 3,000 metres, in light soils and sand.
Family: Crassulaceae.

GREY-LEAVED SUNROSE
Cistus albidus

Erect bushy shrub to 1m high, often less, conspicuous for its hairy grey to whitish stalkless paired leaves, paired 4-6cm leaves, strongly net-veined below. Flowers variable one to four, light mauve, up to 7cm across, branch-terminating. Petals five, crumpled ends, broadly rounded. Stamens centrally bossed, orange yellow.
Habitat: Common throughout the Mediterranean, often forming colonies on calcareous soils in rocky areas, on hills and in light woodland.
Family: Cistaceae.

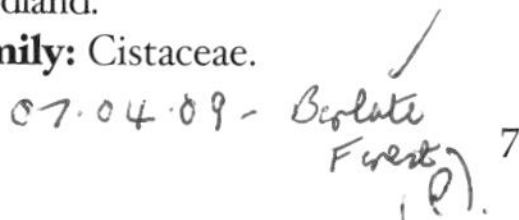

GUM CISTUS

Cictus ladaniferus

Evergreen, tall, lax shrub up to 1.5m high conspicuous for its large, 5-10cm-wide, rose-like, short-stalked flowers, borne on the branch ends, white, with or without maroon blotches at the base of the petals (a feature more common in plants growing in northern Spain). Sepals distinguished by three small swellings. Leaves unstalked, shiny sticky-ladanum above, white-haired below, highly ladanum-fragrant. Gathered commercially, Ladanum is used for the manufacture of perfumes and sticking plasters.

Habitat: Common throughout the Mediterranean, especially in the south of Spain where it is often the dominant plant on low hills.

Family: Cistaceae

HARE'S TAIL

Lagurus ovatus

Distinctive, small to medium, silky-headed soft grass, with the feel and appearance of a hair's tail. Somewhat delicate, hairy annual grass up to 50cm high, stems erect or decumbent. Leaves woolly, shorter than the swollen ribbed sheathes, pale greyish-green. Heads pale silvery brown, oblong to egg-shaped, 2cm long. Spikelets single-flowered, narrow to 10mm long. Glumes hidden within the dense head. Awns 1.5cm long, bent, thin and twisting.

Habitat: Common throughout the Mediterranean, native in the Channel Islands, a casual of the UK, on light soils in dry places, often near the coast.

Family: Gramineae.

HAIRY LUPIN

Lupinus micranthus,
Syn. L. hirsutus

Low to medium height hairy annual. Leaves palmately whorled at the end of short to medium-length petioles. Leaflets oblong, broader above the centre, edges hairy. Flowers deep blue, standards marked white, tip of keel deep purple. Lower flowers alternate, upper in whorls. Pretty but the flowers quickly fall to form brown hairy seed pods. Poisonous.
Habitat: Widespread, on roadsides, in fields, on banks and woodland edges, on acid soils.
Family: Leguminosae.

seen 6·04·08 AFP
11·04·09 " (P)

HALIMIUM

Halimium atriplicifolium

Upright, attractive, small branching shrub to 1m high, bearing thin clusters of bright lemon-yellow flowers, 3cm wide, conspicuously borne on long lateral stalks. Flower stem long, leafless, sivery-haired. Leaves stalked to 3cm long, strongly central veined, silvery grey-green and scaly. Sepals, lanceolate white hairy with a few long reddish hairs. Petals usually falling early in the day.
Habitat: Open woodland, on tracks, dry hills, banks and in shrubby areas, Spain to Morocco.
Family: Cistaceae.

✓AFP Spring 2009 (P).

HAWTHORN, MAY

Crateagus monogyna

A fairly well-known, thorny, deciduous shrub or small tree. Often cultivated in double forms, in pink and red varieties. Widely used agriculturally for hedging purposes, and sometimes in gardens where it provides valuable shelter and food for wild animals and birds. Flowers heavily scented. Distinguished by its fruits, bearing only one seed (stone) per haw. The other hawthorn, C. oxycanthoides, absent from Spain, usually has two stones per haw and flowers about seven days earlier.
Habitat: Common throughout Europe.
Family: Rosaceae.

HEDGE BINDWEED

Calystegia sepium

Vigorous pale green climber, up to 30cm, often more. Stems rapidly twisting and climbing in an anticlockwise direction. Flowers solitary, large, white, attractive, narrow funnel-shaped opening very wide at the mouth, broad trumpet-shaped up to 5cm long on stems about as long as the leaf stems. Bracteoles part-concealing the calyx but not swollen at the base. Leaves large to 15cm long, generally heart-shaped, cordate to triangular, stems shorter than the blade.
Habitat: Widespread throughout Europe, climbing through and into hedges, trees and fences, generally favouring light, damp soils.
Family: Convolvulaceae.

HELIOTROPE

Heliotropium europaeum

A low-growing annual, of spreading or erect habit. Flowers off-white, small, scentless with pale yellow eye, carried to one side of the forked flower stem, the forked tips curling backwards. Leaves medium-green, oval elliptic, held on slender stalks. Insignificant, though widespread, plant flowering over a long period. The rather similar species, H. dolosum, differs in having scented flowers while the blue-flowered, pot-grown ornamental semi-tropical H. officianalis is heavily fragrant and commonly cultivated, especially in the UK.
Habitat: Widespread throughout the Mediterranean on open areas, fallow ground, roadsides and cultivated land.
Family: Boraginaceae.

HEMLOCK

Conium maculatum

Leafy, mousy-smelling annual or biennial, historically infamous for its poisonous properties. Up to 3m high, often less. Stems hollow-grooved, much - branched above, hairless, indiscriminately marked or blotched red-purple. Leaves large, two to four times pinnate, segments toothed. Flowers small white on stalked umbels grouped six to 20, forming broad flat compound umbels. Bracts six, triangular ovate, bracteoles up to six. Fruits globular to 3.5mm across. Poisonous throughout, including its seeds, but the vegetative portion loses its poison when dried.
Habitat: Common throughout most of Europe, on damp ground, near rivers, streams, ditches and soft soils.
Family: Umbelliferae.

HERB ROBERT
Geranium robertianum

A variable hairy perennial, leaves dark to light-green, sometimes reddish, palmate with five-pinnate lobed, long-stalked leaflets below, upper short-stalked three-lobed, ternate. Stems thin, weakish, wiry, often coloured deep rosy-red, spreading or upright, up to 50cm high. Fruit beaked, up to 2cm long, calyx red and hairy. Petals rounded, bright to soft pink, often with one to two narrowly V-shaped, deep pink veins, centre stamens small, bossed, orange. Weakly fetid throughout. The name geranium is much used erroneously for the popular bedding and pot plant, Zonal Pelargonium.
Habitat: Widespread in Europe, coastal up to 850m.
Family: Geraniaceae.

HILL THISTLE
Cirsium echinatum

A low-growing, ground-hugging thistle, bearing attractive, large, dense, silvery-white-haired flower buds and purple flowers. Leaves lobed, undulate, densely or sparsely covered in silvery-white hairs. Lobes tipped with long pale-yellow spines, hairs. Ends of the topmost leaf tend to be a little higher than the flower.
Habitat: Widespread Spain and France, on hills and mountains in grassy fields and rocky areas above 650m.
Family: Compositae.

HOARY MULLEIN
Verbascum pulverulentum

Colourful, glandular-stemmed biennial up to 1m high, flower stems above widely branched into wide-spreading, conical-shaped terminal racemes. Flowers yellow, borne one to five in the axils of the bracts, stems of flowers shorter than the calyx. Leaves large, ascending smaller, oblong ovate, pointed, glabrous below, crenately lobed, undulate, narrowing towards the base. Upper gradually tapering, becoming more or less triangular, pointed and toothed.
Habitat: Native to central and northern Spain, southern Europe, in the UK found only in Devon.
Family: Scrophulariaceae.

HOARY PLANTAIN
Plantago media

Perennial, finely haired. Leaves broad, oval elliptic, short-stemmed or sub-sessile, five to nine-veined, not furrowed. Flowers, whitish to cream, corolla 2mm long, anthers lilac to white, faintly scented.
Habitat: Widespread throughout Europe and temperate Asia on dry limy soils.
Family: Plantaginaceae.

HOLLOW -STEMMED ASPHODEL

Asphodelus fistulosus

Fibrous, rooted perennial to 60cm, usually less. Stems erect simple or well-branched above, hollow. Leaves basal linear up to 5mm across, semi-circular, margins rough. Flowers up to 2cm wide, white, sometimes pinkish, six-petalled (tepals) wide open, starry, in well-flowered spikes. Tepals to 14mm long, blunt-ended, the central vein marked brown or pink. Starchy roots used for glue-making.
Habitat: Widespread throughout the Mediterranean on poor soils, tracks and roadsides, waste land, sparse grassland and rocky places, often in colonies.
Family: Liliaceae.

HORSE MINT

Mentha longifolia

Perenial, tall erect up to 90cm high, weakly smelling.of mint. Stems tough-branched, especially above, roughish to the touch. Leaves up to 3cm long, deep green, ovate, lanceolate, toothed, hairy above, softly grey hairy below, opposite, more or less unstalked. Inflorescence in whorls, crowded into spikes up to 10cm long, spikes somewhat untidy. Flowers small pale lilac, stamens exserted. Stalks and calyx hairy. Fruiting heads becoming spaced after flowering.
Habitat: Widespread throughout Europe, in damp places and dry river-beds.
Family: Labiatae.

HORSESHOE VETCH

Hippocrepis comosa

Woody-based, diffusely branching, low perennial up to 40cm high. Leaves with four to five greyish-green pairs of oblong 5-8mm-long leaflets, collectively up to 5cm long. Flowers bracteate chrome yellow, five to eight in heads borne on slender curved stems longer than the leaves. Heads forming roughly circular patterns. Fruits, horseshoe-shaped, (hence the common name) with curved persisting style.

Habitat: Locally common on limy soils, Britain to southern Europe and the Alps.

Family: Leguminosae.

HOTTENTOT FIG

Carpobrotus acinaciformis
Carpobrotus edulis

Mat-forming with very long trailing stems. Leaves thick, succulent, triangular in section, upright, broader in the middle and slightly glaucous, borne in pairs, to 7-20cm long, bases fused, imaging the pale-yellow-flowered Carpobrotus acinaciformis in habit and appearance, and similarly a garden escape of South African origin. Flowers brilliant, scintillating carmine-pink (C. acinaciformis straw yellow), many linear-petalled, wide daisy-like to 12cm across, borne on thickened stalks and lasting one day only, but abundantly borne from February to June.

Habitat: Widespread along the Mediterranean coast.

Family: Oizoaceae (Mesembryanthemum family).

21.04.09 - ROADSIDE ON N340 near stable

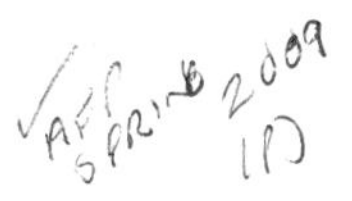

HOUND'S TONGUE
Cynoglossum cherifolium

Small to medium erect, flowering, branched biennial. Leaves distinct, undulate oblong lanceolate, silvery-grey-felted, at first bunched in very lax rosettes, later when flowering half clasping the stem. Flowers 10cm across, pale blue or pinkish, with deeper-coloured net veins, stems slightly arching in bud. Fruits, four-nutted, calyx persistent. Pleasing though not over-attractive plant, occasionally cream-flowered forms found. Common name fancifully refers to the leaves' shape.
Habitat: Widespread in grassland, stony soils, banks and damp areas by streams or ditches.
Family: Boraginaceae.

IBERIS

Iberis pruitii

Low erect or spreading, somewhat fleshy, variable annual or perennial up to 15cm high. Leaves small, spathulate, entire pale green, ends sometimes shallow toothed. Flowers four-petalled in dense globular heads, white or pink, flower stems hardly lengthening in fruit. Fruiting heads (siliquas) strongly notched with two-lobed, outward-pointing wings, up to 8mm long.
Habitat: Widespread through the Mediterranean in rocky crevices on open hills and mountains.
Family: Cruciferae.

JEWELS OF THE MADONNA

Peonia broteri

Because a number of wild plants, shrubs and trees possess attractive, long-lasting, colourful seeds and fruits, they are often cultivated horticulturally. Peonies, apart from their beautiful flowers, also have very showy, colourful seeds, as the illustration portrays. However, they are cultivated for the beauty of their flowers rather than their fruits, possibly because what appear to be scarlet-coloured seeds are in fact sterile bodies which quickly shrivel and lose their colour. (If gathered and dried, some plants, e.g. the stinking iris, Iris foetidissima, retain their colour for long periods.)

Habitat: On low hills and mountains over 500m, in lightly shaded or open areas of southern Spain and Portugal.

Family: Ranunculaceae.

KIDNEY SAXIFRAGE

Saxifraga hirsuta

Spreading low perennial, forming loose, leafy rosettes. Leaves, round to kidney-shaped, cordate at the base, teeth rounded, weakly leathery, both sides with or without hairs, undersides often red-purple flushed. Flower stem leafless up to 30cm high, downy hairy. Flowers small, pearly white, in loose clusters, often once spotted yellow with sparse red spots, ovary pale pink.

Habitat: A plant of cool mountains, absent from the south. Cool, shady rocks and stream sides.

Family: Saxifragaceae.

LAMIUM
Lamium garganicum

Perennial; hairy, spreading up to 50cm tall. Leaves nettle-like, opposite, strongly toothed, cordate at the base, up to 70mm long to 40mm wide. Flowers loosely carried on strong whorled spikes, above or with the leaves. Pale pink to purple, often with darker markings, sometimes white. Corolla tube straight 25-40mm long, slender, mouth wide-gaping, anthers hairy.
Habitat: European mountains, to the Balkans, in hedgerows, on waste land, roadsides and fields. Rare to absent in southern Spain.
Family: Labiatae.

LARGE CUCKOO PINT
Arum italicum, Syn. A. neglectum

A tuberous perennial, at once recognisable by its large, pale whitish-yellow or greenish-white spathe enclosing a large cream-yellow spadix. Small leaves appear autumn, late enlarging, strongly stemmed, acutely lobed, pale green or green-marbled white, up to 30cm long. The pollination system is remarkable. In the cool of evening the spadix burns up sugars growing quite warm, which attracts insects. They descend the spadix, encountering the male and female flowers, thus bringing about pollination. Downward-pointing hairs trap the insects. Within three days the hairs shrivel and the insects are freed. Poisonous.
Habitat: Widespread in shady places Portugal, central and eastern Spain, southern France, UK.
Family: Araceae.

LARGE-FLOWERED BUTTERWORT

Pinguicula grandiflora

Member of an interesting group of insectiverous plants thriving in wet and boggy areas. Leaves more-or-less adpressed, small, yellow-green oval oblong, up to 3-5cm long. Flower usually 8-15cm high, sometimes more. Flowers, corolla bluish violet, conspicuous to 3.5cm long including the short 1cm-long, backward-pointing spur. Lower lip overlapping, sometimes wavy. Upper calyx lip split almost to the base.

Habitat: Local, French Alps, Pyrenees and southwest Ireland, ascending to 2,500m. Trapping and absorbing small insects on the leaves provides additional, possibly much-needed nitrate supplement.

Family: Lentibulariaceae.

LARGE SELFHEAL

Prunella grandiflora

Handsome, conspicuously flowered, violet purple perennial 10 to 30cm high. Flowers, two-lipped, 2.5cm long, violet purple, held in somewhat conical, dense flowered heads. Corolla tube pale, whitish. Calyx divided, upper lip toothed with three equal-length teeth, the lower more or less entire. Leaves, dull green, opposite, oblong to oval, usually blunt-toothed 3-5cm long.

Habitat: Dry fields and meadows, Alps, Pyrenees and Apennines, ascending to 2,400 metres.

Family: Labiatae.

LARGE YELLOW REST HARROW

Ononis natrix

Variable leafy perennial, forming a woody-based, many-branched low bush. Leaves trifoliate, leaflets egg-shaped, sticky pale-green. Flowers large conspicuous-stalked, solitary up to 1.5cm-long, yellow to chrome-yellow, pea-like, showy, clustered in dense, leafy, branched terminating heads. The standard (back petal) veined or streaked, red or violet.

Habitat: Common throughout the Mediterranean on roadsides, banks, rocky areas, sandy soils and scrubland.

Family: Leguminosae.

LAURESTINUS

Viburnum tinus

Smooth-barked, grey-trunked tree, to 3m high, more often a shrub. Leaves leathery, shiny laurel-like, hairy glandular below, rounded to oval entire. Flowers white with five rounded petals and narrow-tubed corolla, borne close in flattish corymbs. Stamens conspicuously projecting. Young branches red-brown hairy. Fruits (mature metal-black, pea-shaped) have been used as a rather drastic cure for dropsy.

Habitat: Throughout Europe, the Mediterranean and North Africa in the garique, woodland edges, and sheltered areas usually near the coast.

Family: Caprifoliaceae.

LAVENDER-LEAVED ROCK ROSE
Helianthemum lavandulifolium

Low to tall erect shrub, height very variable, to 50cm often much less. Distinguished by its bright yellow flowers, 15-25mm across, borne on the ends of the three to five, divided, tightly curled back inflorescence, straightening as the flowers open. Leaves linear, grey-felted, lavender-like, margins revolute, up to 50mm long, giving the plant an overall grey-white appearance.

Habitat: Common in light woodland, light soils, sand areas and the maquis, throughout the Mediterranean.

Family: Cistaceae.

07.04.09 – Borlety ford

LESSER BURDOCK
Arctium minus

Biennial herb, stems tough, to 120cm high. Leaves spirally arranged, large, cordate, softly hairy above, downy grey below. Leaf stems hollow. Flower heads 1-2.5cm wide in short-stalked, small terminal racemes or solitary subsessile in leaf axils, rosy-purple, lower bracts hooked.

Habitat: Widespread throughout Europe, in waste places, field edges and roadsides often in light shade.

Family: Compositae.

LESSER CELANDINE, PILEWORT

Ranunculus ficaria, var. grandiflora
Syn. Ficaria verna

Low-growing, tuberous-rooted perennial, plant. Identified by its shiny, reticulate-veined, glossy, heart-shaped (cordate) leaves and solitary-stemmed, bright yellow star-like flowers. Reproduction is by small bulbils and, to a lesser extent, seeds.
Habitat: Common in damp areas, in sun or part shade. The grandiflora variety is the more common in the Mediterranean area, with larger pale-yellow flowers, usually not so freely borne.
Family: Ranunculaceae.

LESSER MASTERWORT

Astrantia minor

Two easily recognised, similar-flowered, singularly beautiful species, remarkable for their heads of tiny flowers surrounded by conspicuous flower-like white or pink bracts. A. minor is the smaller, with branched stems up to 40cm, the bracteoles free and unjoined. A. major up to 1m with unbranched stems, the bracteoles joined for most of their length. Leaves deeply three to seven-lobed on long stems.
Habitat: Pyrenees, the Alps, up to 650m on calcareous soils.
Family: Umbelliferae.

LESSER PERIWINKLE
Vinca minor

Trailing, prostrate, arching tip, rooting evergreen perennial. Leaves thick, glossy green, heart-shaped at the base, ovate lanceolate, blunt-ended, lightly veined margins hairless, borne oppositely along the stem. Flowers deep blue, up to 30mm wide, corolla tube short, petals wide-spreading. Margins of calyx hairless.
Habitat: Widespread, rocks, streamsides, banks, roadsides, tracks and hedgerows. A garden escape in Britain.
Family: Apocynaceae.

LINARIA
Linaria supina

Distinguished by its blue-green leaves and pale-yellow flowers. Annual or perennial, inflorescences relatively few, up to 10 flowers, pale yellow with orange protuberance on the lower lips. Spur long, not curved, almost as long as the corolla, pale whitish-yellow. Flower stems (pedicels) shorter than the calyx. Stems branching, the base often decumbent.
Habitat: Widespread through Europe but rare in southern Spain.
Family: Scrophulariaceae.

LIZARD ORCHID

Himantoglossum hircinium

Unmistakable thanks to its large, somewhat untidy, flower spike, up to 90cm high, thickly displaying many flowers. Each flower with a long lizard-like "tail" 30 to 50mm long, emitting a smell vaguely reminiscent of goats.

Habitat: Widespread throughout the Mediterranean, but sadly becoming rarer in southern Spain.

Family: Orchidaceae.

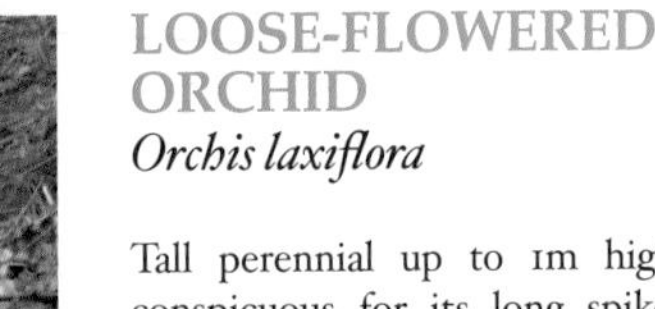

LOOSE-FLOWERED ORCHID

Orchis laxiflora

Tall perennial up to 1m high, conspicuous for its long spikes of well-spaced, deep-wine-red flowers. Basal leaves two to four, erect, shining, green-spotted or maroon blotched, darker below. Stem leaves sheathing, quickly reducing up the stem. Flowers 15-20mm long borne in lax spikes of six to 20, spur rounded, end widening horizontal to slightly upright, shorter than the ovary, bracts three-veined, equalling the ovary.

Habitat: Widespread throughout the Mediterranean in damp places, fields and meadows. A British native, abundant in the Channel Islands.

Family: Orchidaceae.

LONG-HORNED POPPY

Papaver dubium

Variable annual, bristly throughout. Leaves deep green, once to twice pinnate, with narrow, often toothed, segments. Flowers usually without dark central disc or blotches, pale scarlet to 60mm wide. Filaments violet black. Stems with adpressed hairs. Seed pod, long, smooth and glaucous. Not generally quite so profusely flowered or as colourful as the common poppy, Papaver rhoeas.
Habitat: Widespread, roadsides, banks, hedges, on disturbed, cultivated and fallow land.
Family: Papavaraceae.

MAIDENHAIR FERN

Adiantum capillus-veneris

A scaly, perennial rhizomed fern, leaves fresh green delicate, two to four-pinnately lobed, borne on thin, springy black stems. Leaflets fan-shaped held on the thinnest of short wiry stems. The sori (reproductive organs) lie underneath fertile leaves, these bearing protective, recurving edges. Much cultivated for its attractive foliage. Reproduction is by spores, which fall to the ground and develop into tiny, sexually active prothalli.
Habitat: Damp places in shade, by water courses and streams, rock and cliff faces.
Family: Pteridophyta.

MALLOW-LEAVED BINDWEED

Convolvulus althaeoides

Perennial to 1m or more, twinning scrambling climber, sometimes lightly bushy, stems grey hairy. Leaves variable, grey-green to silvery, hairy, the lower generally heart-shaped, the upper palmately five to nine deeply narrow-lobed and divided, the terminal lobe largest. Flowers, large, appealing, deep pink with deeper centres conspicuous, to 5cm across, paired or solitary, stalks longer than the leaves. Cultivated in the UK the flowers are few and weak while growth is rampant to excessive.

Habitat: Abundant through Portugal, southern Spain and the Mediterranean. In dry places, on hills, roadsides and wasteland, through bushes and thickets, and on cultivated land. Seen 12-04-08

Family: Convolvulaceae. AFP

29-03-09- AFP

MANDRAKE

Mandragora autumnalis

Fairly unmistakable rosetted, stemless perennial. Leaves rather unattractive, up to 20cm long, extending later to 40cm, dying away in summer. Crinkly or bullate, wavy-margined, mid-rib dark green. Flowers attractive, short-stalked, mainly centring the leafy rosette, upward-facing five-petalled open bell-shaped. Colour from pink to pale blue. Fruits yellow, globose, fleshy to 2cm across. Reputed to have mystic qualities, with roots in human form. Allegedly can only be uprooted at midnight, when it shrieks pitifully — at other times the molester will surely die.

Habitat: Spain and Portugal, in deserted fields and stony places.

Family: Solanaceae.

Seen Oct 2008 - AFP

MARITIME PINE
Pinus pinaster

Evergreen, two-leaved pine, up to 30m high, individual trees, pyramidal in outline. Trunk red-brown, fissured, boughs darker to grey black. Leaves strong, in stout pairs to 20cm long, deep green, shiny, curved and twisted. Cones up to 18cm long, generally in clusters, strong medium-brown, remaining closed on the tree for many years. Useful timber tree and source of natural turpentine.
Habitat: Common through Portugal and the Mediterranean. Frequently planted, also forms pure forest on light and poor acid soils, more often near the coast.
Family: Pinaceae.

MARSH HORSETAIL
Equisetum palustre

Green, upright, brittle, sometimes decumbent, perennial to 60cm high, usually six to 10 branches, each of which has four to five grooves. Sheaths green, teeth four to eight, blackish, triangular, to 12mm. long. Cones, long, blunt to 30mm.
Habitat: Widespread throughout temperate Europe, Asia, northern Portugal and Spain, North America, in wet areas, bogs, heaths, marshes, wet woodlands, fens and low mountains.
Family: Equisetaceae.

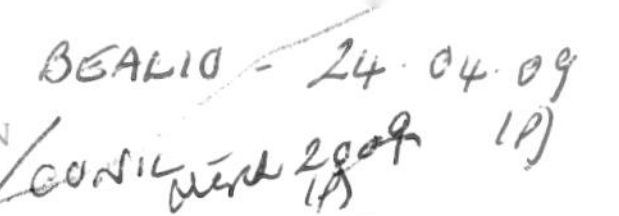

MEDITERRANEAN KIDNEY VETCH
Anthylis vulnerania

Low or ascending, annual or perennial, hairy. Leaves variable, elliptic, leaflets seven to 13, the lower leaves generally single undivided, if compound the terminal leaflet the largest. Stem leaves few and generally equal-sized. Flowers attractive in single or doubly joined, wide-spreading heads, dense, conspicuously green, narrow-lobed, leafy bracted below. Calyx whitish, large, expanded at the base, topped by two large slightly unequal purple teeth. Flowers pale rose-pink, sometimes purpleish.
Habitat: Widespread throughout the Mediterranean, on low hills, dry banks and sparse fields.
Family: Leguminosae.

MERENDERA
Merendera montana

Readily distinguished by its leafless, wide, six-petalled, star-like flowers which appear just above soil or turf level, leaves appearing later. Flowers pale lilac, petals long, strap-shaped with rounded ends, divided almost to the centre, not fused together as in Colchicums.
Habitat: Common throug Portugal, Spain to the Pyrenees, in rocky areas, sparse grass and mountain pastures.
Family: Liliaceae.

MESEMBRYANTHEMUM

Lampranthus roseus

A woody-based, spreading or erect perennial. Leaves succulent to 3cm long, 4mm wide, triangular in section, deep green with minute transparent dots. Flowers eye-catching, brilliant, scintillating carmine, up to 6cm wide, petals narrow, numerous. Centres attractively and plentifully foiled with numerous pale-yellow stamens. Basal stems woody, light brown, flower stems up to 5cm long.

Habitat: Local near the coast, a garden escape becoming naturalised along the Mediterranean on light soils and sand. Widely cultivated. South African native.

Family: Aizoaceae.

MILK THISTLE, HOLY THISTLE

Silybum marianum

A handsome thistle, perhaps more so when out of flower with its large broad adpressed, rosetted, green, strongly marbled white, shiny leaves. Biennial, vigorous up to 1.5m high. Leaves veined or marbled white, pinnately lobed, more-or-less glabrous. Stem leaves smaller, stem-clasping, less strongly lobed, gently spined. Flower heads large, solitary, intense purple up to 40mm across, heads fiercely bracteated, spined, up to 70mm long.

Habitat: Common in the Mediterranean region, in rocky places, waste land, road, tracksides and spoil heaps.

Family: Compositae.

26·04·09 - AFP (P).

MILK VETCH
Astragalus lusitanicus

Perennial up to 1m high erect or spreading, greyish-green hairy, leaflets pinnate, oblong-paired, eight to 12, glabrous above. Flowers vetch-like cream or greenish up to 35mm long, borne in lengthy dense-flowered, but not highly conspicuous, lateral racemes.
Habitat: Local in Portugal and throughout the Mediterranean, in dry areas, banks, roadsides, near pines and in the garique.
Family: Leguminoseae.

MIRROR ORCHID, MIRROR OF VENUS
Ophrys speculum

Low two to six-flowered orchid, up to 25cm high, usually much less, readily distinguished by its deep-blue, shiny, mirror-like flowers and pear-shaped lip, up to 18mm long, narrowly bordered dull yellow with red to black-haired edges. Sepals three small, green, with maroon-red centre-stripe, the upper broader, forming a wide forward-curved hood. Petals very small, deep maroon red. Solitary, or more frequently in very small groups or mini-colonies, often near or in association with the yellow-flowered Ophrys lutea.
Habitat: Widespread throughout the Mediterranean, in dry rocky areas, banks, sparse grass, tracksides and scrub.
Family: Orchidaceae.

MULLEIN
Verbascum sinuatum

Strongly rosetted biennial, leaves adpressed, short-stalked, hairy-felted, whitish-grey or yellowish, undulate, reducing up the stem to triangular to heart-shaped bracts. Stems robust to 2m high. Twiggy branching at the top, branches wide ascending, bearing variously spaced unstalked clusters of deepish chrome-yellow flowers. Stamens five filaments, red violet. Petals fold forward in strong sunshine much reducing their size.
Habitat: Rocky dry places, waste land, pastures, tracksides, fields throughout the Mediterranean.
Family: Scrophulariaceae.

MYRTLE
Myrtus communis

Aromatic shrub up to 3m high. Leaves shiny, leathery, small, ovate to oblong, dark green, with paler undersides. Flowers attractive, up to 2cm-wide, stamens prominent yellow, borne in the leaf axils, providing very effective and picturesque contrast against the dark leaves. A plant associated with ancient romantic Greek and Roman legend. The beautiful nymph Daphne allegedly turned into myrtle to escape Apollo's unwanted attentions.
Habitat: Common throughout the Mediterranean, on dry soils.
Family: Myrtaceae.

NAKED MAN ORCHID

Orchis italica

The flowers fancifully relate to naked men. Spikes tall, dense, up to 60cm high, pyramidal in outline. Flowers pale pink, sometimes whitish, with or without purple lines. Hood forward-pointing. Lip straight, extending downwards, narrow, with two strap-shaped, outward and downward-spreading, arm-like lobes, and two downward-pointing, leg-like lobes below. Between them a very thin, long, pointed tooth. Leaves rosetted, margins sinuate, with or without spots, bracts scale-like.
Habitat: Widespread throughout the Mediterranean in sparse grass, stony places, open woodland and thickets, ascending to 1,000m.
Family: Orchidaceae.

NAKED LADIES

Colchicum lusitanum

A readily distinguished, large-cormed, perennial plant, with large leafless crocus-like flowers appearing in the autumn. Petals (perianth) firm, pink to pale mauve, faint to strongly netted white, mid-vein pale white.
Habitat: Widespread Portugal, through the Mediterranean, among scrub and on rocky ground.
Family: Liliaceae.

AUTUMN NARCISSUS

Narcissus serotinus

Easily recognised, somewhat delicate, autumn-flowering, single-stemmed, lightly fragrant narcissus. Rarely two flowers to a stem, to 25cm high, flowering without leaves. Flowers cream-white, petals (tepals) oblong pointed to 12mm long, corona three to six-lobed, thin, narrow, yellow-gold. Leaves occasionally appearing with the flowers, glaucous, green, 1mm wide to 20cm long.
Habitat: Portugal, Spain, Mediterranean (not France), usually within coastal ranges, in fallow fields, grassy places and light, sandy soils, light woodlands to low coastal hills.
Family: Amaryllidaceae.

NARROW-LEAVED BIARUM

Biarum tenuifolium

Variable, tuberous perennial, immediately recognisable by its striking, unusual, more-or-less stemless flowers, rising leafless out of the ground. Spathes green or chocolate-coloured, erect, sometimes hooded and curved. Spadix deep red to black, projecting well out of the spathe. Leaves after the flowers, long sheathed, spatular-shaped. Reproducing organs in three forms, females below, males above, and above these sterile string-like flowers.
Habitat: Widespread, rocky places, the garique, scrub and meadows.
Family: Araceae.

NARROW-LEAVED HELLEBORINE

Cephalanthera longifolia

Tall, hairless, erect perennial, up to 60cm high. Leaves, seven to 20, lanceolate or linear, ends pointed, shiny, medium green, held upwards and outwards on opposite sides of the stem at 45-degree angle. Flowers, 10 to 20mm across, Madonna white, held five to 20 in loose spikes, sepals and petals forward and inward-pointing, the mouth half closed, upper lip usually faint or more strongly marked orange. Bracts shorter than the flowers.
Habitat: Shady places, under trees and bushes, rocky banks throughout the western Mediterranean.
Family: Orchidaceae.

NOTTINGHAM CATCHFLY

Silene nutans

Woody-based perennial up to 80cm, lower leaves stalked spathulate, upper narrowly lanceolate, softly hairy sessile. Flowers white or pinkish, 18mm wide, paired, drooping, one-sided on sticky stems. Petals narrowly divided almost to the base, two-clawed, white at the centre. Corolla 12mm long. Calyx cylindrical, strongly veined, purple.
Habitat: Widespread, on dry slopes, in fields, hedgerows and stony places, Europe, Alps to more than 2,000 metres, Asia.
Family: Caryophyllaceae.

OLEANDER
Nerium oleander

Evergreen shrub up to 4m high, often forming semi-rounded domes. Branches long, leafy-ended, stiff, generally upright. Leaves dark green, leathery, mid-vein whitish or pink supporting up to 70 thin, lateral opposite-paired veins, sometimes in threes, short-stalked, narrow lanceolate. Flowers large, conspicuous saucer-shaped, bright rosy pink, vanilla fragrant. Petals five rounded, cupping forward at the ends, throat with small petal-like fringed centre. When open, the fruits display thin light-brown, cotton-haired seeds. Damaged leaves exude a poisonous milky latex.
Habitat: Common throughout the Mediterranean, usually around dry water courses, damp places, ravines and steep-sided valleys, forming thickets.
Family: Apocynaceae.

ONOPORDUM
Onopordum nervosum

Vigorous, stiff, strong biennial up to 3m high. Stems stout, broadly winged, fiercely spined. Leaves large, lobed, decreasing up the stem, strongly spined, white veined below. Flower involucral bracts stiffly erect, spiny, heads up to 6cm wide, florets bright pink, longer than the involucral bracts.
Habitat: Hills and mountains, fallow land and cultivations on arid, stony soils. Portugal, southern and central Spain.
Family: Compositae.

OPIUM POPPY

Papaver somniferum

Annual, to 1m high often less, stems and leaves hairless, waxy glaucous.Leaves medium size, sessile, the upper stern clasping, broadly blunt toothed, margins undulate. Flowers large, conspicuous, up to 20cm across. Mauve violet, sometimes white, with or without dark basal blotches. Cultivated, the white flowered unblotched variety is used in the production of salad oils, its black seeds for the decoration of confectionary. The white flowered variety bearing large dark basal blotches is used in the production of codeine, morphine and opium. Its seed are white.

Habitat: Common throughout Europe and the Mediterranean, also pre-sent in the UK. In fields, waste places, spoil heaps and tracksides.

Family: Papaveraceae.

ORCHIS

Orchis mascula, Ssp. olbiensis

A white Mediterranean form of the early purple orchid. Flowers sometimes pink or purple. Stem green, sometimes purple-flushed, leaves with or without purple spots, broad, lanceolate three to five, stem leaves sheathing. Flowers 15-20mm long, generally borne in lax spikes of five to 15, white, or pinkish, sometimes pink or purple, hooded. Lip three-lobed, round-toothed or slightly notched, centre with purple dots. Spur stout cylindrical, curved upwards about the length of the ovary.

Habitat: Europe, North Africa, on grassland, stony areas, the garrigue, banks and hills, in the south limited to mountains.

Family: Orchidaceae.

OROBANCHE
Orobanche ramosa

Parasitic variable perennial, up to 40cm stems, glandular, usually but not always basal-branching, bracts and bracteoles present, stem base often swollen. calyx teeth pointed, shorter than the calyx. Flowers pale blue, sometimes whitish, divided into two lips, the lower with three blunt lobes, the upper with two rounded lobes. Calyx teeth pointed, shorter than the calyx. Wholly parasitic on a wide variety of plants.
Habitat: Throughout the Mediterranean, on fallow, waste and cultivated land.
Family: Orobanchaceae.

OXEYE DAISY
Leucanthemum vulgare

Dark green perennial, up to 1m high, usually much less, roots outward-spreading to form small patches or clumps. Lower leaves stalked, oblong spathulate with softly rounded teeth, stem leaves clasping, sessile teeth more pointed. Flowers large, white, conspicuous daisies up to 10cm across, borne solitary, or on branched, ridged stems. Ray florets (petals) strap-shaped, lightly ridged, white with bluntish ends, central disc broad medium-yellow. Commonest of all daisies, sometimes called moon or dog daisy.
Habitat: Common through Europe, except the south, in fields, hedgerows, below old walls.
Family: Compositae.

PALE MALLOW

Lavatera trimestris

Annual tall, erect, roughish, with large orbicular, medium-green, stalked leaves, base deeply cut, heart-shaped, slightly fanned at the veins, broadly toothed, the upper less so, lobes three to seven, shallow, rounded. Flowers large attractive up to 7cm across, solitary on short stems, broadly baggy epicalyxed below, petals shining satin pink sometimes white, lightly veined deep pink. Stamens prominently bossed cream-white.
Habitat: Common through Portugal, the Mediterranean, on light sandy soils, roadsides, fields and tracks, usually in coastal areas. Widely cultivated, especially in Britain.
Family: Malvaceae.

PALLENSIS

Pallensis spinosa

Easily recognised by its dull yellow flowers, 2cm wide, broad central disc,short-petalled surround and wide ring of star-like, green, hairy spine-tipped bracts twice as wide as the flowers. Leaves, lower oblong, narrowed at base to form a stalk, upper sessile, lanceolate, hairy, grey green in colour. Annual or biennial up to 1m high. Heads narrow or widely branched.
Habitat: Common in dry places, fields, open woodland, roadsides and rocky places.
Family: Compositae.

PALO VERDE
Parkinsonia aculeata

A small, slender, evergreen tree up to 4m high, notable for its long, pendant, tough, deep-green, shiny, alternate pinnate, attractive rather different "leaves". A botanist's delight. The "leaves" are considered to be modified bracts (phyllodes), the true leaves being reduced to a group of three, rarely more, minute leaflets at the base of the phyllodes. Flowers, usually abundant, showy chrome-yellow, stamens and stigmas conspicuous and protruding.
Habitat: A garden escape, native to South America and Mexico, widely planted in frost-free countries for its showy flowers.
Family: Leguminosae.

PAMPAS GRASS
Cortaderia selloana

Easily recognised by its large, silver plumes and thin, hard leaves with sharp, serrated edges. Female plants bear the finest plumes. Hardy. Penetrating the pampas in its native land can be painful experience for animals and humans alike. Needs care in order when handling to avoid painful lacerations from the sharp, saw-like leaf edges. Previously known as C. Argentea, a name which would appear to better reflect the silver quality of the plumes.
Habitat: Treeless plains of South America, particularly Argentina. A garden escape.
Family: Gramineae.

PAPER WHITE NARCISSUS
Narcissus papyraceus

Readily distinguished by its pure-white fragrant flowers, bunched two to 15 to a stem. Petals narrowly ovate, corona, to 4mm long. Flowers November to April. Leaves erect, glaucous, 7-15mm wide. Much used commercially, providing forced flowers for the Christmas market.
Habitat: Widespread throughout the Mediterranean, on roadsides, in rocky places, grassland and meadows.
Family: Amaryllidaceae.

PARONYCHIA
Paronychia capitata

A strange plant, a perennial which carpets the ground with what appear to be silvery grey-white flowers, on closer examination revealed as silvery heads of globular bracts surrounding the real tiny flowers within. The outer sepals with recurving ends, inner shorter. On first sight, could hardly be mistaken for a member of the familiar carnation and pink family.
Habitat: Widespread on rocky roadsides, light soils and sand, hills and mountains, throughout the Mediterranean.
Family: Caryophyllaceae.

APRIL 09 - AFP to CONIL (P)

PEACH-LEAVED BELLFLOWER
Campanula persicifolia

Tall to medium glabrous, attractive, herbaceous, erect perennial, unbranched, up to 40cm high. Leaves dark-green, lower, stalked, oval lanceolate, bluntly toothed, upper narrow, linear. Flowers conspicuous, in lax spikes, blue, sometimes white, up to 40cm wide campanulate, outward-facing to erect, not nodding. Calyx sharply linear-toothed to half the length of the flower.
Habitat: Widespread through Europe, in fields, hedgerows, rocky areas, and cultivated land.
Family: Campanulaceae.

PENNYROYAL
Mentha pulegium

Strong-smelling hairy perennial herb, prostrate at first, becoming strong-spreading erect. Flowers, pale lilac clustered wreath-like around the stem in dense distinct whorls, without a terminal flower head. Pungent smell. Leaves short-stalked, small, to 1cm long oblong to oval, lightly glandular, teeth distant. Bracts similar, reducing up the stem but longer than the flowers. Exterior of corolla haired, glabrous within.
Habitat: Widespread in damp and seasonally wet areas on light and sandy soils.
Family: Labiatae.

PENNYWORT, NAVELWORT
Umbilicus rupestris

A glabrous pale-green, long-stalked, succulent fleshy plant, distinguished by its orbicular (round) leaves with central navel depression and long, usually solitary, spikes of pale-green flowers. Spikes more than half the length of the supporting stem. Upper leaves gradually becoming smaller with crenate or toothed margins.
Habitat: Dry walls, bases of old houses, rocks, cliffs, old bridges and mountain areas, tends to prefer shade.
Family: Crassulaceae.

PENTAGLOTTIS
Pentaglottis sempervirens

Readily recognised by its appealing, bright-blue, white-throated flowers with an inside-out appearance. A bristly haired, vigorous perennial. Leaves elliptic, upper sessile, stem-clasping, light green, strongly alternately veined, leaf margins hairy. Flowers small up to 7mm wide, displayed in leafy branching clusters, bright sky-blue, scaled white at the throat.
Habitat: Through northeast Portugal, central and northern Spain, southern France. Prefers shady damp places, near hedgerows and woodland edges.
Family: Boraginaceae.

PEONY
Paeonia broteroi

Rhizomatus, bushy perennial up to 35cm high, bearing large, attractive carmine-red flowers, up to 12cm across wide-opening. Leaves divided into leaflets 17-20 shiny deep-green, hairless below. Stems tinged red. Stamens conspicuous yellow with pale-yellow filaments (stalks). Follicles (ovaries) three to five, usually hairy.
Habitat: Woodland edges, scrub and rocky areas.
Family: Ranunculaceae.

PEONY
Paeonia coriacea

Tuberous perennial up to 50cm high, readily distinguished by its large hairless leaves, dull green above, pale grey beneath and large, 10-15cm, silver-pink flowers, bossed with numerous golden stamens. Leaves twice divided (2 x ternate) into elliptic leaflets, leathery. Flowers usually with two carpels hairless, tapering to a point. Flowers resemble large pink tulips. Due to its beauty the plant is often pulled out, but Paeonies are notorious for transplanting badly.
Habitat: Local in southern Spain, open areas, woodland edges or light scrub.
Family: Ranunculaceae.

PERENNIAL SPURGE

Euphorbia characias

A sturdy shrub-like perennial bearing green, brown-centered, cup-like flowers borne in wide floriferous whorls terminating the tops of hairy, 30-80cm-high woody stems. Leaves dark green narrowing at the base, lanceolate, leathery, bunched thickly towards the tops of the stems. Spurges exude a milk-like latex when damaged, said to irritate the skins of allergic persons.

Habitat: Local in dry hills and mountains and stony areas, Spain to Morocco.

Family: Euphorbiaceae.

PHLOMIS

Phlomis crinita

Perennial, large shrub-like plant distinctive in its leaves and stems covered in dense silver hairs and somewhat broad, clumsy, close whorls of large flowers, corolla 2.5cm long. Unusual in their brown-yellow shade, carried strongly on the stem. Bracts, narrow hairy. Leaves, oval-lanceolate or lanceolate, young leaves silvery white, older leaves less so, untoothed, strong thick to leathery, stalks short, abrupt. Young plants form attractive lax rosettes of pure-white leaves.

Habitat: Common in southern and eastern Spain, on low hills and mountains in open, stony places.

Family: Labiatae.

PHLOMIS
Phlomis lychnitis

Low white-felted, evergreen, single-stemmed, erect or spreading sub-shrub. Leaves narrow, woolly, white-felted, five or six times longer than broad. Flowers yellow 20-30mm whorled, four to eight whorls to the stem, held in oppositely paired, broad, felted, cup-shaped pointed bracts.
Habitat: Dry rocky areas, woodland edges, the garrigue and open shrubland, Spain to southern France.
Family: Labiatae.

PHLOMIS
Phlomis purpurea

Dwarf evergreen shrub of lax growth, but can attain 2m height in good conditions. Flowers in distant whorls above each other with eight or fewer flowers to a whorl. Large, pink to pinkish purple. Bracts hairy, soft, unspined. Leaves stalked, lanceolate, grey-green above, white felty below.
Habitat: Common to central and southern Spain, on low hills, banks, scrub and rocky places.
Family: Labiatae.

Seen 06-04-08 A.F.P.
29-03-09 AFP
07-04-09 - Berlute Fische
(PHOTOS)

PINE CONE KNAPWEED

Luezea conifera

A perennial, unusual in the shape of its cone-like flower heads up to 30cm high carried on strong, erect, usually leafy, whitish-haired stems, heads often solitary. Leaves deep green, white-felted below, white-hair flecked above entire or cut into broad blunt lobes. The small flowers rise from the top of the 2.5 to 3cm-long cone of narrow egg-shaped heads formed of overlapping papery bracts, corollas small white, pale pink or light purple.

Habitat: Locally common, Portugal, Spain to Italy, in light pine woodland, heath, the garique, on rocky areas and uncultivated land, lowlands to mountains.

Family: Compositae.

PINK BUTTERFLY ORCHID

Orchis papilionacea

To my eye the most beautiful of the native orchids. Flowers pink, up to 10 in loose spikes on short, strong stems, pink-veined, streaked or dotted, crimson, purple or violet. Leaves narrow, grooved, sheathing up the flower spike.

Habitat: Widespread on low dry hills, in grassland and scrubland.

Family: Orchidaceae.

BARBATE
LA BREÑA 29.04.09
(P)

PITCH TREFOIL
Psoralea bituminosa

Perennial, usually lightly branched to 1m high with dark green trefoil leaves, the lower with somewhat rounded leaflets, the upper narrowed to a point, more-or-less glabrous throughout. Flowers an unusual, dull blueish-lilac shade, loosely held in roundish, open clover-like heads 10 to 15 on long stalks, a closely appendaged tooth bract below. Calyx teeth narrow-pointed, hairy, slightly shorter than the flowers. Mature fruit pods beaked, outward-spreading, to 15mm long. Said to smell strongly of tar when crushed, hence the name.
Habitat: Throughout the Mediterranean in dry areas, track and roadsides, banks and thickets.
Family: Leguminosae.

PLANTAIN
Plantago lagopus

Annual, rosetted, leaves lanceolate, erect, medium-green, three to five-veined, stalks much shorter than the flower stalks. Flowers many, heads silvery compact, 1cm by 2cm, solitary, on shallow, furrowed stalks up to 40cm long. Stamens conspicuous cream, filaments, corolla, bracts and sepals all silvery-haired.
Habitat: Widespread throughout the Mediterranean, on dry soils, banks, roadsides, waste, fallow and cultivated land.
Family: Plantaginaceae.

3[illegible].03.09 CONIL

POLICEMAN'S HELMET
Impatiens glandulifera

Tall, robust annual up to 2m high. Stems stout, fleshy, somewhat translucent, light green, often tinged red. Distinguished by its large 4cm-long flowers of unusual, not unattractive bean-like shape, resembling a policeman's helmet. Corolla roundly tubed, opening at the mouth with two sepals, the lower broad, divided and short-spurred. The upper rises towards the back of the corolla, upright, large, forward-pointing, with pointed end. Borne five to 10 on long, thin peduncles rising from the leaf axils of the upper leaves. Leaves stalked, lanceolate, up to 15cm-long, serrate, accuminate held opposite or in whorls of three, becoming smaller up the stem.
Habitat: Native of the Himalayas. Naturalised throughout Europe in damp places, by streams and river banks.
Family: Balsaminaceae.

POMEGRANATE
Punica granatum

Low, deciduous, lightly spined bush to small tree, up to about 5m high, frequently much less. Leaves short-stalked, bright, fresh green, shiny above, oblong, entire and opposite. New shoots four, angled. Flowers a bright shade of vermilion red, centred with a conspicuous boss of yellow stamens, petals five to nine, crinkled. Fruit large, highly coloured in shades of red brown, edible pulp around the large seeds. Used as an astringent against tapeworms. Also a fertility symbol.
Habitat: Naturalised throughout the Mediterranean.
Family: Punicaceae.

PICTURE OF FRUITS
LA BREÑA BARBATE
APRIL-09 (P)

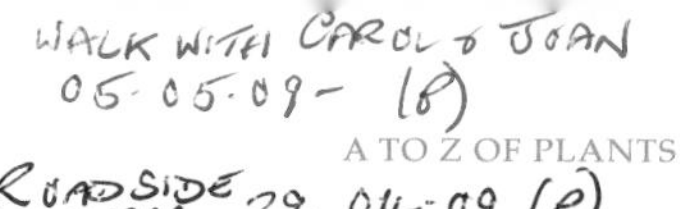

PRICKLY PEAR, BARBARY FIG

Opuntia ficus-indica

Introduced into Spain from the Americas, reportedly by Columbus. The large, white aerioled, spiny blue green stem pads are at once recognisable. Flowers and filaments yellow, petals scintillating, held above the green, egg-shaped, spiny fruit, maturing yellow-red. Fruits edible, sometimes available in markets.
Habitat: Common on dry, stony ground, by roadsides and tracks.
Family: Cactaceae.

PROVENCE ORCHID

Orchis provincialis Ssp. pauciflora

Perennial, short to medium up to 20cm high, rarely up to 40cm. Leaves shiny, lax rosetted below two to five, narrow lanceolate-pointed, stem leaves sheathing the lower stem. Flowers yellowish, spurred, large to 25mm long, three to eight in erect spikes. Petals and sepal wide-spreading, with the rear sepal broadly triangular, stiffly erect. Lower lip prominently three-lobed, bright yellow centred deep orange. Spur curved upwards, broad-ended.
Habitat: Poor soils in light shade on grassy banks, open woodland, the maquis and the garrigue.
Family: Orchidaceae.

PURPLE VETCH

Vicia benghalensis

Variable bluish-green annual or short-lived perennial up to 80cm high, distinguished by its rosy-purple flowers, black at the tips. Leaves once pinnate, leaflets in pairs of four to 12, linear oval. Flowers on long stems, part pendant in spikes equal to or shorter than the leaves.

Habitat: Widespread throughout the Mediterranean on track and roadsides, waste land, field corners and the base of walls.

Family: Leguminosae.

PUTORIA

Putoria calabrica

Alpine-like plant forming wide evergreen mats. Leaves small, to 1cm long, leathery, margins downward-curling, rolled under. Flowers abundant, small, corolla to 1.5mm long, white, sometimes tinged pink, four-petalled with four long, diagnostic, protruding anthers. Stamens tinted red or pink.

Habitat: Habitat, dry rocks in mountains, throughout the Mediterranean, not France.

Family: Rubiaceae.

PYCNOCOMON
Pycnocomon rutifolium

A tall, robust, erect perennial up to 1.75m high. Stems much-branched. Flowers white-cream or pale yellow, part round to globose or flattish, inner florets smaller than the outer, involucral bracts below fused, cup-shaped, all held upright on thin wiry stems. Leaves thickish, fern-like, gradually reducing upwards into bracts, the lower sometimes entire. Despite its size has dainty appearance.
Habitat: Widespread throughout the Mediterranean, but local on sand dunes and sandy areas near the sea.
Family: Dipsacaceae.

QUAKING GRASS
Briza maxima

Slender appealing grass with inverted, plump, silver-chaff-coloured, corn-like pendulous spikelets daintily set on thin, wiry stems. A slender few-stemmed annual to 45cm high, solitary or more usually gregarious, leaves few, flat, hairless. Flowers in loose sparingly branched heads, spikelets 25mm long to 15mm wide. Glumes finely haired, attractively overlapping, broadly boat-shaped, silver-chaff-coloured, sometimes purple-tinged at the base. Often dried for ornamentation.
Habitat: Widespread throughout the Mediterranean, Spain, naturalised UK, light soils, meadows, tracksides and woodland edges.
Family: Gramineae.

RAMPING FUMITORY

Fumaria capreolata

A deceptively delicate-looking plant with blue-green, fern-like leaves and whitish or pale pink flowers tipped dark red-black. Annual, very short to tall, spreading and scrambling sufficient at times to completely envelop supporting high plants, or shrubs. Leaves ferny, small glaucous, segmented into blunt-ended, wedge-shaped lobes. Flowers up to 20, borne on stalked racemes, racemes shorter than their stalks, corolla tube 14mm long.
Habitat: Common throughout the Mediterranean and Europe on cultivated, fallow land, hedges, fields, waste areas, spoil heaps, walls and bridges.
Family: Fumariaceae.

RED-BERRIED MISTLETOE

Viscum cruciatum

Semi-parasitic plant found on olives, almond and hawthorn trees. Usually close to tight, opposite-branching, colour yellowish-green throughout. Stems and leaves glabrous, thick. Leaves borne opposite in pairs, veins three to seven parallel. Flowers in small short-stalked inflorescences, small, green four-petalled. Male and female flowers separate, stamens quickly falling. Fruits, succulent pea-size red berries with viscid centers, ripening November, December. Not used festively in Spain, as is the white-berried mistletoe, V. album, of Britain, France and northern Europe.
Habitat: Southern Portugal and southern Spain.
Family: Loranthaceae.

ROCK MARIGOLD

Calendula suffruticosa

Spreading, woody-based, medium-green perennial up to 40cm high, often supporting itself by growing through the perimeter of thin low shrubs. Leaves slightly fleshy, glandular, hairy, sparsely shallowly toothed, short-stalked or sessile, upper sessile. linear lanceolate or oblongish, ends pointed. Flowers up to 40cm across, rays (petals) yellow, broadly linear, ends rounded up to 35 a head, disc slighly darker than rays. Backs of outer ring of fruits usually spiny.

Habitat: Portugal, southern Spain (rarely inland), North Africa and Greece, in dry places, rocky areas and sands near the sea.

Family: Compositae.

ROSEBAY WILLOW HERB, FIREWEED

Chamaenerion angustifolium syn. Epilobium angustifolium

Colourful, patch-forming, vigorous, herbaceous perennial, up to 120cm high. Unmistakable for its long spikes of rose-purple flowers, followed by curved, mature-fruiting heads, quickly opening to reveal thinly whitish silky-covered seeds. Leaves dark green, spiral, narrow oblong, lanceolate, both ends narrowed, margins often undulate. Blue-green below, strongly veined. Petals in fours, uneven, one pair larger than the other. Calyx deep purple. Stigmas on older flowers recurved. The name "fireweed" refers to its rapid colonisation of bomb sites during World War Two.

Habitat: Roadsides, disturbed ground, woodland clearings, hedgesides and rocky places, absent southern Spain. Native to central Europe, Asia and North America.

Family: Onagraceae.

ROSEMARY

Rosmarinus officinalis

Pleasantly aromatic, evergreen, twiggy, erect perennial shrub, reaching up to 2m, sometimes spreading and lower-statured. Glabrous, leaves leathery, dark green, paler below narrow linear to 3.5cm long, margins rolled under. Flowers lavender blue, sometimes darker, rarely white, in narrow stem terminating spikes. Corolla, two-lipped, up to 1.5cm long, lower lobe broad-ended, calyx two-lipped, downy. Flowers most of the year. Oil-producing, an ingredient of cologne, and said to contain antiseptic and insecticidal properties.

Habitat: Portugal and the Mediterranean area on dry calcareous soils, low hills and the littoral.

Family: Labiatae.

ROSY GARLIC

Allium roseum

A smooth, hollow-stemmed bulbous member of the onion tribe. Variable, 15 to 40cm high. Flowers in rounded umbels, pale pink, sometimes white, with or without bulbils. Flower bracts two to four-lobed, shorter than the flower stalks. Leaves all basal, four to six, edges finely serrated.

Habitat: Widespread on light soils, hills and grassy rocky places, often in scattered colonies.

Family: Liliaceae.

ROUND-HEADED LEEK
Allium sphaerocephalum

A tall, slender, bulbous perennial, readily distinguished by its globular dense head of black-purple flowers, with two sub-tending, papery bracts below. Stamens protruding. Leaves, two to six, the upper side slightly grooved. A white variety also occurs.
Habitat: Widespread on roadsides, fallow land, cultivated and waste land.
Family: Liliaceae.

ROUND-HEADED RAMPION
Phyteuma orbiculare

An extremely difficult genus, many species similar and flower colour varies. In addition, botanically confused by several authorities applying names to different species. Herbaceous perennial, basal leaves rosetted, toothed, stalked, triangular to heart-shaped, ascending less stalked, upper leaves sessile, lanceolate, stem-clasping. Flowers blue to steel-blue in globular or flattish heads, surrounded below by long, broad, lanceolate, irregular star-forming bracts.
Habitat: Mountains up to 2,500m, north, central, northeast Spain, the Pyrenees.
Family: Campanulaceae.

ROWAN, MOUNTAIN ASH
Sorbus aucuparia

Deciduous tree up to 20m high, attractive in flower, more so in fruit. Crown narrowing branches tending to ascend a little upwards. Leaves pinnate. Leaflets seven to nine, borne opposite in pairs, all leaflets roughly the same size, lanceolate oval oblong, entire dark-green glabrous above. Flowers corymbose, numerous, woolly on shortish stems, cream-coloured. Petals, small oval. Fruit round, scarlet, pea-size, mature bunches heavily drooping and conspicuous.
Habitat: Central Portugal, UK, Spain to Russia, the Caucasus, Moroccan mountains. Grows up to the levels of 2,600m, higher than any other deciduous tree.
Family: Rosaceae.

RUSH-LEAVED JONQUIL
Narcissus juncifolius

Bulbous perennial similar to the familiar common jonquil, except the flowers are one or two per stem with a larger corona. Leaves dark green, slender, rush-like, corona (cup) deep yellow, half as long as the yellow, spreading perianth (petal) segments. The common jonquil, N. Jonquilla, is a plant of damp areas and meadows, bearing up to six flowers per stem with a smaller corona. It is highly fragrant and commercially used in perfume manufacture, particularly in France.
Habitat: Native, through Portugal, south and central Spain to north Africa, naturalised in France and some areas of the Mediterranean, rocky areas in hills.
Family: Amaryllidaceae.

RUSTY-BACK FERN
Ceterach officinarum

Unmistakable small, evergreen fern of dry rocks in full sun. Leaves (fronds), pinnate, short, brown scaly, sessile, or short-stalked up to 20cm long, thick, grey green, leathery, wide linear, shape, overall oblong. Leaflets, short, broad-based, slightly unopposite, or overlapping at the lower edge, rounded, edges thinly scaled, cream-white. Undersides silvery white as fronds unfold, maturing to brown and scaly. Scales partly hiding the spore-bearing sori.
Habitat: Widespread, through the Mediterranean, Europe to the Himalayas, on dry walls, houses and roofs, in rock crevices.
Family: Polypodiaceae.

SAFFRON CROCUS
Crocus sativus

A cultivated plant, rarely escaping to the wild, though the very similar wild saffron crocus, C. cartwrightianus, occurs wild in Greece. Both distinguished by their very long, orange-red styles, usually protruding well outside the flower. Flowers autumn, large, deep to pale lilac, petals conspìcuously veined purple, often fusing the base, all purple. The styles (the ends divided into three in the wild species) are laboriously gathered to provide culinary saffron. Yellow stamens provide the inferior yellow saffron.
Habitat: Though mainly cultivated, escapes to fields, fallow land and neglected gardens.
Family: Iridaceae.

ST. BARNABY'S THISTLE

Centaurea solstitialis

A tall, 20-60cm high, white, sparsely cottony annual, almost non-spiny thistle, with buds and flowers heavily armed with outward-radiating golden spines. Basal leaves deeply toothed, upper lanceolate, spine tipped, decurrent to the stem below.
Habitat: Widespread in fields and cultivated light soils, mainly Europe and the eastern Mediterranean.
Family: Compositae.

ST. BERNARD'S LILY

Anthericum liliago

Bulbous perennial up to 60cm tall. Leaves grey-green, basal hairless, narrow up to 7mm wide, roughly half the length of the flowering stem. Flowers greenish-white, star-like, up to 3cm across, few on long spikes, bracts small linear, much shorter than the flower stalks. Petals six, narrowly oblong. Style curving, stamens attached at base. Similar at first glance to asphodel.
Habitat: Widespread on stony places and grassland.
Family: Liliaceae.

ST. DABEOC'S HEATH

Daboecia cantabrica

Immediately recognisable by its pleasing rosy-pink, 8-12mm, nodding, lantern-like flowers, daintily borne on thin, wiry stems, seven to nine to a stem. Leaves, linear, dark green above, margins revolute, white-hairy below, 5-10mm long. Plant, somewhat unkempt, shrubby heath-like, height up to 50cm, stems thin, straggling.

Habitat: Cool places on acid soils, native to north, central and western Spain, northwest Portugal, western France, parts of Ireland. A garden escape on British heath.

Family: Ericaceae.

SAND SEDGE

Cyperus capitata

A rather inconspicuous, tough, blue-green, low-creeping plant. Flowers, a little obscure and more interesting than colourful, appear from the sand as if from nowhere. Leaves few, outward-spreading with deep, inrolled margins, often becoming light brown or deep maroon-coloured. Spikelets, deep to light brown, borne in small solitary heads, without rays. Bracts three to four erect and leaf-like, extending well beyond the flower head.

Habitat: Widespread in sandy, coastal areas.

Family: Cyperaceae.

SAND SPURREY
Spergularia rubra

Wide-spreading or semi-erect annual or perennial, leaves narrow linear in cluster-like whorls, axils with sharp stipules. Stems swollen-jointed. Flowers usually profuse, mauve-pink, 4-6mm across sometimes to 1cm, fully open, sepals silvery, variable, often nearly as long as the petals.
Habitat: Common throughout Europe on non-saline sand or light gravelly and cultivated soils.
Family: Caryophyllaceae.

SAWFLY ORCHID
Ophrys tenthredinifera

A delightful, early flowering orchid, readily distinguished by its three broad, bright pink-to-carmine sepals, green-lined in the centre, and its large, brown, hairy, outward-spreading lower lip, diagnostically broadly edged yellow-green, the lower part split into two by the upturned protuberance. Centres marked with two short, bluish, oblong, white-surrounded markings. Lower leaves broad, upper leaves upright.
Habitat: Widespread in dry grassy areas, the base of shrubs, between rocks, woodland edges, the maquis and garique along the Mediterranean coast, south and central Portugal.
Family: Orchidaceae.

SCABIOUS
Scabiosa stellata

Easily recognised by its appealing, large, spherical, 2-3cm-wide, fruiting heads of silvery pale-straw-coloured, papery, frilled bracts. Annual, stems spreading, greyish-green, roughly haired. Basal leaves much divided, cut or deeply toothed, stem leaves broadly lanceolate, segmented into long, linear pointed segments. Flowers pale lilac 3-4cm wide in flattish to semi-rounded, silvery-haired heads. Inner florets shorter than the petalled outer. Calyx usually five-bristled. Seed heads conspicuous globus papery crowns with five basal stars.

Habitat: Spain, France to Turkey, in dry areas, banks, grassland, waste places and roadsides. S. cretica, native to the Balearics, Sicily and Italy, bears similar fruiting heads with purple flowers.

Family: Dipsacaceae.

SCORPION VETCH
Coronilla juncea

The rush-like, upright, grey-green, pithy, stiffly straight stems readily distinguish this rather thin, small-branched shrub, up to 1m high. Flowers yellow in close umbels of four to eight, borne on stalks longer than the leaves. Leaves sparse, with opposite lobes of three to seven linear leaflets. Fruits, four, angled, jointed.

Habitat: From Portugal to western Spain and North Africa, in dry soil on hills, light woodland tracks and roadsides.

Family: Leguminosae.

SCORZONERA

Scorzonera crispatula
(see also Viper's Grass)

Handsome tuberous perennial with large, dandelion-like, dark-centred flowers up to 5.6cm across, borne solitary on strong erect stems up to 30cm high, often branched below. Involucral bracts shorter than the ligules. Leaves variable, crispy, glossy green above, up to 23cm long, oval oblong or spathulate, margins undulate, thinly spinned. Stem leaves few, much reducing up the stem, sessile. Closely related to the cultivated so-called "edible vegetable oyster", S. hispanica.
Habitat: Portugal, southern, central and eastern Spain to southern France, on dry, rocky, open ground, track and roadsides, low inland hills.
Family: Compositae.

SEA DAFFODIL

Pancratium maritimum

Immediately recognised by its large white, daffodil-like, sweet-scented flowers, borne on strong stems up to 40cm high usually rising from the dead or dying foliage. Most attractive when in flower. Leaves broad, up to 20mm across, erect, robust glaucous. Bulbs large, often protruding from sand, or deeply buried. Fruit, a large, glaucous, three-lobed, egg-sized capsule. Seeds large, black.
Habitat: Maritime dunes, especially wind-blown sand.
Family: Amaryllidaceae.

SEA LAVENDER
Limonium sinuatum

Easily distinguished perennial with deep green, usually three-winged upright stems to 50cm, and rosetted wavy-edged lanceolate leaves. Flower heads flat, elongated, bearing conspicuous mauve-coloured calyx, centred with small white true flowers. The whole plant rough to touch.
Habitat: Widespread in the Mediterranean area, usually near the coast, on light sandy soils, rocky areas, track and roadsides.
Family: Plumbaginaceae.

SEA ROCKET
Cakile maritima

Annual greyish-green herb, up to 45cm erect or sprawling, stems thick, tough, hairless. Lower leaves deeply irregularly pinnately-lobed, toothed or untoothed, 3-6cm long. Upper entire or lobed, smaller, sessile. Flowers four-petalled, 6-14mm-long, borne in dense stem-terminating racemes, pale lilac to white or deep mauve. Racemes unattractively elongating in fruit. Fruits (siliquas) pale brown-green to 25mm-long conspicuously jointed on to short thick stalks.
Habitat: Europe and the Mediterranean on coastal sand and shingle — readily floating fruits and seeds remain viable in salt water for long periods.
Family: Cruciferae.

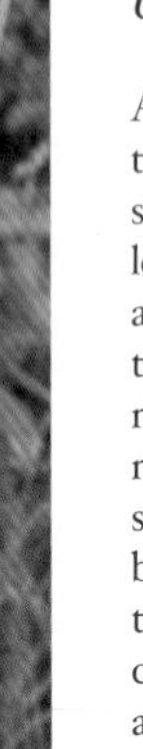

SEA SQUILL, AUTUMN SQUILL

Urginea maritima

At first sight similar in general aspect to asphodel, bulbs very large, but sea squill is autumn-flowering, without leaves, usually making rapid, robust appearance from driest of soils to mature quickly. Sometimes solitary, but more often in thick to sparse colonies. Flowers white, borne in dense spikes, flowering upwards from the base. Petals white, brown-nerved, anthers protruding. Buds silvery white, conspicuously brown-nerved. Leaves appearing with ripening fruits, large, shiny, bright green up to 80cm long to 10cm across. An extremely poisonous plant, used in the treatment of heart disease. A North African form is used to make rat poison.

Habitat: Sands, dunes, rocky areas and dry hills not far from the sea, throughout the Mediterranean.

Family: Liliaceae.

SELF HEAL

Prunella vulgaris

Short, rhizomed perennial up to 30cm high. Stems dark green to red-purple, erect, with or without sparse hairs. Leaves short-stalked, oval, dark green, shiny above, bluntly toothed or entire. Flowers blue-violet, occasionally white or pink. Calyx and bracts with short white hairs.

Habitat: Common throughout Europe, the northern hemisphere and Australia, in coppice, woodland glades and clearings, grassland, wasteland and tracksides on neutral soils.

Family: Labiatae.

SHEEP'S BIT

Jasione montana

Attractive flowered plants but a very difficult genus. Flowers held on almost leafless, glabrous stems, up to about 30cm high, involucral bracts, shorter than the flowers. Upper leaves medium-green, small, oblong undulate, lower leaves larger, toothed.

Habitat: Widespread through Portugal, Spain, Europe, in sparse grass, waste areas and tracksides.

Family: Campanulaceae.

SHEPHERD'S NEEDLE

Scandix pecten-veneris

A short, hairless variable annual, leaves two to three times pinnate, lobes narrow linear, toothed. Flowers tiny, borne in small leaf-opposing umbels, whitish aspect. Outer flowers often a little larger, up to 2-3mm long, rays usually bractless. Secondary bracts often present, hairy. Fruit rather egg-shaped, beak upright, very long, needle-like up to 80mm long, borne in small clusters, usually with the remains of a few dead flowers at the ends (said to resemble the wool on a shepherd's needle).

Habitat: Widespread through Europe, Mediterranean to the Himalayas, in fields, rocky hillsides, fallow and cultivated land.

Family: Umbelliferae.

SHRUBBY HARE'S EAR

Bupleurum fruticosum

Tall evergreen shrub up to 2.5m. Stems upright, slender, leaves borne at fairly even intervals, dark green, usually broader above the middle, tough leathery, central vein strong, whitish. Flowers in small-to-large, wide umbels of five to 25 spreading rays, yellow-green or yellowish. Bracts reflexed, narrow, oval, veined, five to seven, soon falling away. Fruits narrow small-winged.

Habitat: Southern Europe and Mediterranean, on roads and tracks, the garique and stony places. Often cultivated.

Family: Umbelliferae.

SHRUBBY PIMPERNEL

Anagallis monelli

Low, semi-erect, spreading or mat-forming, hairless perennial, basal stems woody, otherwise green, slender, rounded. Leaves small, linear ovate, up to 1cm long, pointed, opposite or whorled, unstalked. Flowers abundant, conspicuous, up to 3cm, brilliant sky-blue, on slender stems much longer than the leaves. Stamens tufted, rose, purple-white or blue. Flowers only open in full sun, vividly striking in full flower.

Habitat: Through Spain to North Africa, on dry sands, roadsides, bare waste places and sparse grass.

Family: Primulaceae.

29.03.09 AFP BARBATE
13.04.09 BREÑA (P)

SHRUBBY THYME

Thymus capitatus

A dwarf, dry, crisp-looking shrub, unpleasant to the touch except when bearing its ample flower heads, these in clusters at the end of short leafy stems, in pink, purple, occasionally white shades. Old leaves brittle as stems become dry, and spiny to the touch. New leaves pleasingly aromatic, hairy, soft, linear to 9mm long, 2.3mm wide, mid-green, small thyme-like, whitish felty beneath. Flowers 4-6mm long, stigmas protruding, borne in small clusters, separating at maturity. Calyx finely bristle-haired.
Habitat: Widespread Spain and southern Europe on dry limy soils, banks and roadsides, dry hills, embankments and rocky areas.
Family: Labiatae.

SHRUBBY TOBACCO

Nicotiana glauca

Lax silver-grey, branched, hairless shrub or small tree to 5m. Leaves stalked, tough glaucous-green, alternate oval to lanceolate, pointed. Flowers green-yellow, corolla long tube 4cm long, mouth narrow-opening to five abrupt very narrow petals, borne few to many in long lax panicles. Calyx five-toothed, in fruit becomes papery and persistant papery fully enclosing the flower tube base and seed capsule.
Habitat: Native to South America. Naturalised throughout the Mediterranean, on wasteland, old walls, rocky-stony areas, track and roadsides.
Family: Solanaceae.

SICILIAN SNAPDRAGON

Anthirrinum siculum

Perennial, hairless except for the glandular inflorescence. Short to medium height, stems upright, branched, usually leafy at the stem axils. Leaves entire, medium-green, narrow elliptical or linear, below opposite, alternate above. Flowers up to 25mm long, pale yellow, base rounded, not spurred, mouth closed, palate broadly marked deeper yellow, sometimes veined red.
Habitat: Naturalised in Spain, native to southwest Italy, in rocky areas, on old bridges and walls.
Family: Scrophulariaceae.

SILENE

Silene colorata

Attractive, spring-flowering hairy annual, up to 30cm high, often in numbers. Flowers bright pink, loosely clustered to one side of the stem. Petals deeply divided almost to the base. Calyx, hairy, strongly veined purple. Lower leaves 1-3cm long, narrow-stalked, broader towards the apex. Upper narrow lanceolate.
Habitat: Widespread throughout the Mediterranean, except France, on sandy light soils near the coast.
Family: Caryophyllaceae.

SILVER SAGE
Salvia argentea

Biennial to perennial, stems square, much branched above into opposite widespreading, flowering stems. Basal leaves short-stemmed, large in adpressed rosettes, oval-oblong, strongly rugose, margins large-toothed. Meridian vein strong, whitish. Flowers white, sometimes flushed pink or pale yellow, widely two-lipped, the upper strongly upward-forward-curved, lower blunt rounded. Corolla up to 35mm long. Fairly easily recognised due to its candalabra-like head, large white flowers and adpressed rugose leaves.
Habitat: Throughout Spain to Italy, on rough stony ground in hills and mountains.
Family: Labiatae.

SLENDER BROOM RAPE
Orobanche gracilis

Parasitic perennial, rarely up to 50cm high, medium to slender, wholly reddish glandular, hairy. Flowers yellowish with deep red to blackish-red lips, shiny, deep reddish within. Lower lip with three equal lobes, stigma yellowish-purple-edged. Scale leaves oval lanceolate. Fields and woods rocky areas on legumes, cistus and some grasses.
Habitat: Mainly eastern Mediterranean.
Family: Scrophulariaceae.

SMALL-FLOWERED GORSE

Ulex parviflorus

Evergreen, very spiny, usually abundantly flowered, honey-fragrant shrub, rarely up to 1.5m. Shoots with long terminal spines up to 30mm long. Stem spines usually shorter, bent or straight. Leaves (phyllodes) alternate on the stem, small 0.5cm-long, spiny. Flowers yellow, two-lipped, toothed, upper with two teeth, lower three. Calyx brown-yellow, hairy at first.
Habitat: Common in dry rocky areas, coast to mountains, Portugal to France and the Balearics.
Family: Leguminosae.

SMALL-TONGUE ORCHID

Serapias pseudocordigera

Narrow-leaved orchid, up to 50cm high, usually less. Leaves splayed outward, pointed, channelled. Flowers to 3.5cm long, colours obscure, dull pink and brown-red shades, carried four to 10 on strong stems. Bracts prominent, exceeding the flowers, pale pink with deeper parallel veins. Hood triangular, greenish, lip reddish-pink, broad-pointed, hairy.
Habitat: Throughout the Mediterranean, in damp areas, banks, hills, marshes aand shrubby areas.
Family: Orchidaceae.

SNAPDRAGON
Anthirrhinum graniticum

Tall conspicuous flowered perennial, erect or occasionally climbing. Flowers in long spikes, white, sometimes very pale pink, mouth pale orange bossed, up to 32mm long, shortly stalked to 15mm long. Leaves ovate to oblong lanceolate, alternate above, opposite below. Fruits glandular, hairy, to 10mm long.
Habitat: Through central and northern Portugal, central and southern Spain, on old walls, rocky areas and stony hillsides.
Family: Scrophulariaceae.

SNAPDRAGON
Anthirrhinum majus

Readily recognised, bearing dense, handsome, terminal spikes of deep rosy-pink flowers, sometimes paler, with prominent, yellow, bossed lips. Spikes on vigorous plants up to 1.5m high. Leaves, dark green, oval, usually hairless. Cultivated in many coloured, hybrid forms.
Habitat: Old walls and bridges, dry rocks and rocky areas, widespread throughout the Mediterranean. Well known as a garden bedding plant UK.
Family: Scrophulariaceae.

BARBATE LA BREÑA
29.04.09 (P)

SOAPWORT, BOUNCING BET

Saponaria officinalis

A stoloniferous perennial up to 90cm high. Flowers in flattish, compact corymbs at the head of leafy glabrous stems, pink or off-white, 2.5cm wide. Calyx long, to 18 or 20cm, teeth short, triangular, often reddish towards the tips. Leaves, oval elliptical, acute, glabrous, veined 3-5. The five-petalled flowers reminiscent of a narrow-petalled form of garden phlox.

Habitat: Widespread, Europe, damp places by streams, ditches, hedges, roads and bank sides.

Family: Caryophyllaceae.

SOFT RUSH

Juncus effusus

Stiffly erect, mat-rooted, shiny, glossy, green-stemmed perennial, up to 1.5m high, usually covering areas in wide tufts and patches. Stems, soft, interior pithy throughout, smooth or very faintly furrowed. Leaves reduced to dull reddish-brown basal sheaths. Inflorescence lateral, approximately one-fifth downwards from the tip of the stem, shortly lax or rounded into a single head. Flowers brownish-cream.

Habitat: Abundant throughout Europe and parts of the southern hemisphere, frequently dominant in wet marshy areas.

Family: Juncaceae.

SOMBRE BEE ORCHID, DULL ORCHID

Ophrys fusca

Perennial up to 40cm, usually less, flowers three to six, easily recognisable due to the two large, blue, "eye-like" spots prominently situated at the top of the almost black lower lip. Petals and sepals pale yellow-green broad to narrow, strapshaped. Leaves pale green, basal broadly lanceolate, ends rounded, stem leaves linear lanceolate, pointed. Due to its colouring, often difficult to spot. There are three subspecies with fairly minor differences.
Habitat: Common throughout the Mediterranean, in sparse grass, open rocky areas, and light shrubby places on calcareous soils.
Family: Orchidaceae.

SOUTHERN VETCHLING

Lathyrus tingitanus

Glaucous, climbing annual, sometimes scrambling to 1m high or more. Leaves paired opposite at the end of winged stems, upper narrower two to four, with solitary terminal tendril. Flowers conspicuous, large, deep magenta-purple, up to 4cm wide, carried one to three on long stems. Flowers showy, completely scentless, sweet-pea-like. Calyx teeth equal in length. Whole plant hairless, fruiting pods beaked, shiny when ripe.
Habitat: Common through Portugal, western Mediterranean to Morocco and North Africa, in dry places, banks, low hills, waste and scrubland.
Family: Leguminosae.

SPANISH BLUEBELL
Scilla hispanica

Readily distinguished robust, attractive, bulbous perennial up to 50cm high, often less. Leaves broad, shiny, bright green, 10-35mm across. Few to many-flowered. Flowers, pale blue, held erect or more usually outward-facing, wide-mouthed, campanulate, not nodding or with recurved tips. Anthers blue.
Habitat: Widespread Portugal to Italy, in mountains and along the Mediterranean, in fields, rocky places and cultivated land.
Family: Liliaceae.

SPANISH BROOM
Spartium junceum

Evergreen bush, up to 3m high, generally leafless, the small simple leaves quickly discarded. Branches stiff, dark-green, upright to partly spreading, long, thin, round in section, rush-like. Flowers profuse, conspicuous, bright yellow, pea-like 2cm long, solitary within terminal spikes. Seed pods black when ripe. Strongly pineapple- scented. Stems can be used for basket-making, the flowers for yellow dye. Has diuretic properties.
Habitat: Widespread throughout the Mediterranean in dry areas, banks, roadsides, woodland edges and the maquis.
Family: Leguminosae.

DAFFODIL, SPANISH DAFFODIL

Narcissus hispanicus

A large-flowered, deep yellow daffodil, readily recognised by its mono-coloured flowers, twisted petals and leaves. Flowers 5.5cm long, perianth segments (petals) twisted. Leaves twisted 7-12mm broad, glaucous.

Habitat: Native to south and north of Spain including Pyrenees, in damp areas, fields and stony places.

Family: Amaryllidaceae.

SPANISH IRIS

Iris xiphium

A handsome, flowering, bulbous perennial which may attain a height of 60cm, usually less. Flowers conspicuous, purple blue to violet, falls marked bright orange-yellow, petals more or less of equal length. Leaves long and narrow, shorter than the flower stem, up to about 5mm wide, pale glaucous. Tends to grow in small colonies, but sometimes solitary. Flowers break off easily.

Habitat: Local in areas generally near the sea, in wet-winter places, on heavy soils, fields, rocky areas and woodland edges, Spain, France to North Africa.

Family: Iridaceae.

BARBATE
LA BREÑA - 29.04.09
(P)

SPANISH MOUNTAIN THISTLE

Ptilostemon hispanicus

Attractive if formidable perennial, rosetted until flowering stage begins, up to 1m high. Leaves, deep green, shiny, whitish below, mid-vein yellowish, formidably armed with long golden spines. Flowers large, up to 36mm wide, in few-flowered cymes, pale blue, surrounded by rays of fierce, strong upward, outward and downward-spreading spines, attractively tinged deep rose-purple, tipped straw colour.

Habitat: High places, mountains usually over 400m on and between rocks, tracksides and rubble in limestone areas, southern Spain.

Family: Compositae.

SPANISH RUSTY FOXGLOVE

Digitalis obscura

A sub-shrub, up to 1m high, unmistakable for its large orange-yellow to orange-brown, sometimes dull-to-obscure-coloured flowers, darkly net-veined inside, with lower lip protruding. Leaves narrow linear, shiny above forming basal rosettes before flowering.

Habitat: Open rocky areas in full sun, southern to central Spain.

Family: Scrophulariceae.

SPINY GLOBE THISTLE
Echinops strigosus

Annual up to 50cm. Immediately recognised by its spiny leaves, thrice-pinnate, grey-green, bristly and unpleasant to handle. They bear attractive, 4-8cm-wide, silvery-blue globular heads of flowers.

Habitat: Dry soils, banks and roadsides southern to central Spain and Portugal.

Family: Compositae.

SPOTTED ORCHID
Orchis maculata

A solid-stemmed plant, variable in height, stature and flower markings. Leaves greyish-green-spotted, six to 10, ascending, spaced wide up the stem into bracts, shorter than or equal to the flowers, sometimes longer. Spike pyramidal at least until the top flowers mature. Flowers rose to white, lower lip broad, three-lobed, coloured with purple dots or lines. Outer petals spreading, spur round, straight. The sub-species O. fuchsii and O. ericetorum are somewhat similar.

Habitat: Widespread in Europe and around the Mediterranean, mainly in hilly areas on acid soils, on roadsides, hedgerows, woodlands and heaths.

Family: Orchidaceae.

SPOTTED ROCK ROSE, ANNUAL ROCK ROSE

Tuberaria guttata

Conspicuously flowered, highly variable annual rock rose, distinguished by its yellow flowers 10 to 20cm across, maroon-blotched at the base, narrowly ringed red above. Height, variable, small to medium. Flowers solitary or branched, fruits downward-pointing. Leaves, broadly lanceolate, with or without hairs, basal rosette persisting during the flowering period.

Habitat: Widespread throughout the Mediterranean in open areas, light woodland, sandy or light soils, sand dunes, the maquis and fields.

Family: Cistaceae.

SPURGE LAUREL

Daphne laureola

Readily distinguished, small-branched evergreen shrub to 1m high. Leaves shiny, pale green, laurel-like up to 15cm long, tending to congregate at the top of the branches. Flowers up to 12mm long, pale green, held five to 10 in small axillary racemes amid the topmost leaves. Corolla opening to four petals. Fruits small, black, shiny drupes, up to 12mm across.

Habitat: Widespread, though locally common, throughout Europe in woods and shady places. Poisonous.

Family: Thymelaeaceae.

SQUARE-STALKED ST. JOHN'S WORT

Hypericum tetrapterum

Perennial, variable in height, erect to spreading, semi-prostrate but more usually upright. Stems squarish below, narrowly four-winged. Leaves sessile, medium green, obovate to oblong, with minute translucent glands. Flowers three-styled, numerous, bright yellow up to 12mm wide, borne in a wide, lax, spreading panicle. Sepals with two black glands.
Habitat: Widespread through Europe, in damp places, meadows, fields open woodland.
Family: Hypericaceae.

SQUILL, SCILLA

Scilla peruviana

Unmistakable for its many-flowered, spiral cone of blue to purple-blue, sometimes pale-blue, flowers surrounded by broad, glossy, ground-hugging, rather fleshy leaves. A bulbous perennial squill. The specific name is a misnomer, the plant at one time considered to have originated in Peru. Widely cultivated for the beauty of its flowers.
Habitat: A true Mediterranean plant, native to damp rocky areas, tracksides, light scrub, grass, shrub and woodland edges.
Family: Liliaceae.

SQUIRTING CUCUMBER
Ecballium elaterium

A sprawling, bristly-haired, non-tendrilled fleshy plant spreading outwards to 60cm or more. Leaves large, coarse, palmate to triangular, base heart-shaped, green, paler below. Flowers yellow or pale-yellow, small, borne in the axils of the leaves, males on slender racemes, females usually solitary. Fruits cylindrical up to 6cm long, conspicuous, hairy, bent backwards when ripe. Poisonous. Ripe fruit explodes, squirting the seeds some distance. Used medicinally in controlled form against some serious diseases.
Habitat: Widespread in the Mediterranean area, on dry banks, tracksides, dumps and waste land.
Family: Cucurbitaceae.

STAR CLOVER
Trifolium stellatum

Little resembling the common clovers we generally recognise, but readily distinguished due to its spherical fruiting heads which ripen to become red-brown, opening and forming distinctive pale white-centred stars. A low-spreading plant. Flowerheads rounded, covered by the long silky calyx hairs. Flowers small, pale pink, about the length of the calyx teeth, later wide-spreading to become star-like. Leaves small with three clover-like (trefoil) leaflets, oblong, toothed.
Habitat: Common in dry places throughout the Mediterranean, on roadsides, sparse fields, waste places on light soils and sands.
Family: Leguminoseae.

STAR OF BETHLEHEM

Ornithogalum narbonense

Bulbous perennial. Leaves, four to six, spreading, slightly channelled, bluish-green persistent throughout the flowering period. Many flowers, forming pointed spikes upwards on the long stem up to 60cm high, star-like, white, to 36mm across. Outward facing fruits adpressed against the stem. Tepals six, strongly veined, green on the reverse. Bracts up to 2cm long, green, extending past the flower buds. The name Star of Bethlehem is popularly used for at least three other plants.

Habitat: Widespread throughout the Mediterranean, in fields, fallow and cultivated land, tracksides, banks and low hills.

Family: Liliaceae.

STAR THISTLE

Centaurea calcitrapa

Variable perennial, very low-spreading to quite high, stems grooved, much branched. Leaves greyish-green, narrow lanceolate, pinnately lobed or almost entire, lower broader, tending to die away as the plant matures. Flowers mauve, small, rather thistle-like, up to 8mm across, surrounded by long, spined, whitish-yellow star-like bracts, sometimes additionally spined towards the base.

Habitat: Dry places, roadsides, sparse grassland, rocky areas, sandy soils, fallow and cultivated land.

Family: Compositae.

STINKING HELLEBORE

Helleborus foetidus

Robust perennial herb. Fairly easily recognised by its numerous, large, pale green, round to bell-shaped pendant flowers, tinged reddish at the base to 3cm wide. Also by its large, evergreen, coarse, strongly stemmed palmate leaves, borne from the stem. Segments variable, narrow to broadly lanceolate and pointed, dark green, the upper paler than the lower. The whole smelling strongly fetid, especially when gathered, roughly disturbed or bruised.
Habitat: Widespread, Spain, Italy, UK, on calcareous soils in light shade, woodlands, banks, bushes and tracks.
Family: Ranunculaceae.

STONECROP, WALLPEPPER

Sedum acre

Low, mat-forming, succulent, glabrous evergreen perennial. Stems creeping to upright. Leaves sessile bright green, fleshy succulent, alternate, small to 5mm long, drying papery at the base. Flowers terminal, conspicuous, five bright yellow petals, widespreading, lanceolate to 12mm across borne on small two to four flowered branches. Often cultivated in rock gardens or used as an edging plant in Britain.
Habitat: Common throughout Europe, including mountains of southern Spain, usually on calcareous soils, rocks and old walls.
Family: Crassulaceae.

SUNFLOWER
Helianthus annuus

Well-known, readily distinguished plant. Mono-cultivated for its oil-producing seeds and animal fodder, when its large flowers turn fields brilliant yellow, early summer. Said to be gyroscopic, but is not always so. Frequently escapes to the wild on roadsides and sometimes back to gardens.
Habitat: An escape from cultivation, found alongside roads and tracks and in fallow fields in dry sunny places.
Family: Compositae.

SWEET ALISON, SEA ALLYSUM
Lobularia maritima

Small, low, deeply rooted annual or perennial herb, flat-spreading or, scrambling through adjacent plants on ascending weak stems up to 30cm high. Leaves dense to few, somewhat silvery-haired, dark green, narrow, linear 2-4cm long, sub-sessile. Flowers four-petalled, 6mm across, rounded, on compact semi-globular heads. Chalk-white, sometimes flushed pink, fragrant. Long flowering, January to August, with odd flowers throughout the year. Widely cultivated in highly fragrant, white, pink and purple dwarf coloured forms.
Habitat: Widespread throughout the Mediterranean on light sandy soils and rocky areas, generally near the sea.
Family: Cruciferae.

BARBATE - LA BREÑA
29.04.09 (l)

SWEET CHESTNUT
Castanea sativa

Well-known, fairly familiar, wide-spreading deciduous tree, frequently cultivated for its edible nuts, borne 1-3 in large, soft, pale-green, spiny husks. Leaves large, lanceolate to oblong, edges lightly toothed, shiny above, light scaly below. Flowers in conspicuous wide-spreading rays of cream-yellow catkins, male flowers above, females below, heavily fragrant. Induces hay fever in sensitive persons.
Habitat: Through France, Spain, northern Portugal and Italy.
Family: Fagaceae (oak family).

TALL BEARDED IRIS, FLAG
Iris germanica

A distinct, vigorous, variable, rhizomatus iris, up to 1m high with large 10cm-wide, unmistakable, fragrant, violet-blue flowers, held two to three on strong stems. Perianth (petals) in threes, outer falling outward, purple veined with prominent yellow or whitish, centred beard, inner curved inwards. Spathes papery above. Leaves broad, sword-shaped, strictly upright, light glaucous green, shorter than flower stems. Rhizomes thick, light-loving, exposed above the ground.
Habitat: Widespread, in dry places throughout the Mediterranean.
Family: Iridaceae.

TAMARIX

Tamarix hispanica,
Syn. T. africana

Black to purple-black-stemmed, woody shrub up to 3m high, usually much less. Flowers in pink or white feathery racemes, up to 6mm wide, 30 to 60mm long, borne on the previous year's wood, accompanying the new season's leaves. Leaves small, adpressed to stem, 1.5-6mm long, papery margins visible when dry. Easily recognised, but differenciating between species can prove difficult. Bedouin tribesmen obtain food from a desert species, T. mannifera, which could be the manna mentioned in the Bible.
Habitat: Widespread in western Mediterranean, in damp places and near the sea.
Family: Tamaricaceae.

TASSEL HYACINTH

Muscari comosum

Bulbous plant up to 15cm high, easily recognised by its heads of upward-pointing, blue flower buds, brown-blue and turning downwards when in flower, outward-pointing and green-brown in fruit. The whole surmounted by an upright, conspicuously colourful, stemmed tuft of violet-blue infertile flowers. Leaves, upright to flat, five to 17mm broad, three to 17mm long, tapered at the ends.
Habitat: Widespread throughout Europe in fields, banks, fallow and cultivated land.
Family: Liliaceae.

31-03-09 - Conil
(P)

TEASEL

Dipsacus fullonum

Tall erect perennial, up to 1m high. Stems angled, angles spined, upper less so, or without spines. Leaves rosetted at first, lower large-spined with fused bases, upper less spined, sometimes spineless. Heads large, oblong, egg-shaped, consisting of many green-flushed, pinkish or purpleish, spined bracts centred with tiny pink or lilac flowers. Heads drying out in fruit, becoming hard, resilient dark brown-silvery in colour. The dried heads are used for teasing wool.

Habitat: Widespread in temperate Europe, in damp places, by streams and waterways.

Family: Dipsacaceae.

THISTLE, COMMON THISTLE

Galactites tomentosa

Erect annual up to 1m high, often less. Leaves deeply lobed and spined, white-marked along the veins, rosetted at first, later spreading upwards to form leafy branched stems, winged towards the base. Flowers 2cm across, pale to purplish pink, nodding, borne slightly to one side of the stem. Outer flowers spreading to form a star-like halo effect, the inner smaller forward-pointing.

Habitat: Widespread in the Mediterranean, on light soils, dry banks, waste places, track sides.

Family: Compositae.

THORN APPLE

Datura stramonium

Erect, coarse, opposite-branching herb up to 1m high. Leaves large, to 20cm long, dark metallic-green, coarsely jagged lobed. Flowers large to 15cm long, borne in the upper leaf or stem axils, white, sometimes purple, tube-shaped, ends barely opening, with five outward-spreading, long, thin teeth. Calyx pale green, teeth five, angled, broad, pointed to almost half the length of the corolla. Fruit chestnut-like, pale green, densely spined, occasionally spineless, to 5cm long. Very poisonous (if ingested, $3/20^{th}$ of an ounce is reported to create a feeling of vitality, 6/20th to cause madness, 9/20th permanent insanity and 12/20th certain death).
Habitat: Widespread throughout the Mediterranean, on disturbed ground, spoil heaps and waste land.
Family: Solonaceae.

THORNY BROOM

Calycotome infesta

Fiercely spined shrub, up to 2m high, spines strongly broad-based, laterally borne, straight and long, ends very sharp-pointed. Branches alternate, young branches smooth, hairless. Leaves many short-stemmed, small trifoliate, comprising three obovate, quickly falling leaflets. Flowers, highly fragrant, golden yellow, solitary or in twos or fours, stalks two to three times longer than the calyx. In full flower a glorious shrub. In colonies forms bright yellow-gold carpets wonderfully, perfuming surrounding areas.
Habitat: Widespread around the Mediterranean, on acid soils in dry sunny places, on banks, low hills, road and tracksides, rocky areas and the garique.
Family: Leguminosae. Fabaceae.

TRIQUETROUS GARLIC
Allium triquetrum

A bulbous perennial. Triangular flower stems, up to 40cm long, combined with attractive panicles of white, bell-shaped flowers, without bulbils, and green-veined petals immediately identify this plant. Leaves two to five, bright green, slightly succulent, narrow linear, with prominent mid-vein. Flowers, in lax, drooping panicles, later more erect, three to 15, held somewhat to one side of the stem. Individual flower stems (pedicels) longer than the flowers. Smells strongly of garlic if crushed.
Habitat: Shady moist banks, meadows and fallow land, Portugal, southern Spain to Morocco and Italy.
Family: Liliaceae.

THROATWORT
Trachelium caeruleum

Perennial, up to 75cm high, usually less, distinguished by its wide profusely flowered corymbose (flat heads) of flowers in an appealing shade of blue, rarely white. Individual flowers tube-like, bearing five small, outward-spreading petals and long projecting styles, all very tiny. Leaves variable, dark green, narrow to broad, with saw-toothed edges.
Habitat: Common in south, southwest and central Spain and Portugal on old walls and bridges and rock faces, usually in shade.
Family: Campanulaceae.

12 04-09 AFP (P)

THYME-LEAVED SPEEDWELL
Veronica serpyllifolia

Appealing small eyebright, flowered weed of cultivation. Easily distinguished by its white to pale-blue flowers, to about 1cm wide, and the triangular-shaped corolla, lined above in blue violet or dark slate colours, 30 or less borne in long, lax, terminal racemes. Leaves pale green, up to 2cm long, oval oblong, ends rounded, lightly crenulate, passing up the stem into bracts. Stems ascending into flowers, creeping nodal rooting, lightly hairy.
Habitat: Found in moist places, fields, hedgerows, wasteland and heaths, common Portugal, central and northern Spain, northern Europe, Asia to South America.
Family: Scrophulariaceae.

TOLPIS
Tolpis barbata

Annual, usually diversely branched up to 40cm high, branches more or less leafless. Readily distinguished by its pale-yellow, deeper yellow centred flowers up to 30cm wide, discs brown purple with below, slender pointed bracts forming a fine involucral ruff. Leaves, deep green, glabrous above, linear to broad lanceolate, sometimes shortly lobed and toothed.
Habitat: Spain, Morocco in dry areas, fallow and waste land, the garique, on sandy and light soils.
Family: Compositae.

APRIL 09 QAFP (P) – OUTSIDE HOME!

TRAGOPOGUM
Tragapogum hybridum

Biennial, to 50cm, readily distinguished by its small central rose-violet or lilac flowers surrounded by eight narrow, long, pointed, green, star-like bracts up to 40mm across. Petals (rays) few or none, sometimes up to five, always much shorter than the bracts. Stems soft hairless upright solitary or sometimes branched to 50cm. high. Leaves linear, broader at the base, long, pointed, bluish. Seed heads large, conspicuous, with wind-blown seed-distributing parachutes.
Habitat: Portugal, Spain and southern France, in grassy fields, roadsides, thickets and hedges.
Family: Compositae.

TREE GERMANDER
Teucrium fruiticans

Thin-spreading, woody, white-stemmed shrub up to 2.5m high, usually much less. Distinguished by its paired, pale blue flowers, stamens protruding, the lower lip large with five to seven lobes, more usually five, the central lobe the largest, up to 2.5cm long. Leaves opposite, bluntly ovate, green above, white felted below.
Habitat: Widespread in the Mediterranean area and south-west Europe, in the garrigue, rocky banks and dry areas, generally near the coast.
Family: Labiatae.

29.03.09 AFP (P)

TREE HEATH

Erica arborea

Evergreen shrub up to 4m high, reputed to assume tree form in the Azores. Leaves profuse, tiny 0.5cm long, in whorls of three along the stem. Young growths haired white. Flowers profuse in terminal pyramidal clusters, small white 2-3mm long, bell-shaped, sometimes flushed pink. Anthers conspicuous brown, not protruding. E. Lusitanica, native to Portugal and northern Spain, is similar, but with flowers up to 5mm long, usually pink. Leaves, twice size of those of E. arborea.
Habitat: Widespread in the Mediterranean area, on acid soils, in woodlands, hedge sides, scrub and heathland, ascending to about 650m.
Family: Ericaceae.

TURPENTINE TREE

Pistacia terebinthus

Deciduous shrub, sometimes tree-like, up to 2.5m high. Leaves short-stalked,compound (rose-like), paired four to five leaflets with a terminal leaflet, shiny dark green, untoothed. Flowers, compound in branched clusters, brownish, petal-less, largely inconspicuous. Anthers and stigma dark plum-coloured. Fruits attractive red, quickly turning brown, pea-sized. The bark produces a fragrant sweet gum.
Habitat: Abundant throughout the Mediterranean, Portugal and North Africa, on dry hillsides and gullies, in woods, rocky areas and the maquis.
Family: Anacardiaceae.

UPRIGHT MIGNONETTE

Reseda alba

Readily recognisable by its long, narrow spikes of creamy-white flowers, whorled intermittently and irregularly up the stem. Leaves with five to eight narrow, deep, unequal, lobes and wavy margins. Flowers cream-white, to 9cm wide, petals and sepals five, seed pods four, toothed.

Habitat: Widespread throughout the Mediterranean, in rocky places, sparse grass, roadsides, banks, sandy places and around old bridges and walls.

Family: Resedaceae.

VETCH

Vicia dasycarpa

Climbing or scrambling, bushy annual, sometimes untidy in habit, up to 2m high, conspicuous with its many racemes of small, downward-facing blue to purple flowers, occasionally tinged white or yellow. Leaves pinnate, leaflets four to 12 paired, dark green, hairless, end tendrils small, branched. Racemes usually longer than leaves. Vicia villosa is similar though more hairy, as the name suggests.

Habitat: Roadsides, fields, scrubland, waste areas and the garique. Naturalised over much of the Mediterranean.

Family: Leguminosae.

Seen 12·04·08 A.F.P.

VIOLET

Viola alba, Ssp. dehnadtii

Low-spreading plant, stolons non-rooting. Leaves tufted, deep green, heart-shaped with or without hairs, margins round, crenately toothed. Flowers violet or mauve-violet, perfumed, lateral petals with white throat hairs, spur short upward-turning. Fruits glabrous or hairy.
Habitat: Widespread on mountains, not the coast, absent from the eastern Mediterranean, in shady, moist areas, hedge sides, rocky areas and streams.
Family: Violaceae.

VIOLET CABBAGE

Moricandia arvenesis

A short-lived, medium-to-tall, branched perennial, basal leaves, smooth somewhat fleshy, much resembling small cabbage leaves. Upper, sessile, heart-shaped, stem-clasping, blue-green in colour. Flowers in spreading racemes terminating the stems, violet with darker centre, petals four, wide-spreading, up to 20mm long.
Habitat: Common throughout the Mediterranean on calcareous soils.
Family: Cruciferae.

VIOLET LARKSPUR

Delphinium peregrinum

A delightful, generally low-growing, variable annual larkspur, occasionally up to 50cm high, bearing conspicuous deep blue-violet, flowers, with spurs twice the length of the flower, ends slightly upturned. Leaves lower dissected, broadly ferny, upper entire, sparse. Stems, whitish hairy, stiff, upright. Delicate-appearing but remarkably tough, withstanding unshaded summer sun.

Habitat: Common throughout central and eastern Mediterranean, in dry, light soils, sand, rocky areas and fields.

Family: Ranunculaceae.

VIPER'S BUGLOSS

Echium vulgare

Erect variable annual or biennial, one or many-stemmed, rough-haired, medium height. Leaves oval lanceolate, upper part stem-clasping, lanceolate to narrow linear, bristly-haired. Flowers sub-sessile in short elongating cymes. Corolla blue to 19mm long, haired, open-mouthed funnel-shaped, stamens four to five, protruding.

Habitat: Widespread in Europe, and the Mediterranean, in open areas on light soils, sand dunes, cliffs and grass.

Family: Boraginaceae.

seen 12·04·08
AFP

VIPER'S GRASS

Scorzonera graminifolia (see also Scorzonera crispatula)

Perennial, up to 45cm, leaves glaucous, linear, entire, to 3mm wide, numerous, base slightly sheathed, ascending the stem to terminate just below the flower head. Flowers pale yellow, conspicuous up to 4cm wide, 5cm long, closing shortly after midday. Involucral bracts, inner-pointed, long, narrow, linear to bluntly triangular. The flowers, paler coloured than most of this genus, mature to form magnificently engineered seed-distributing parachutes.
Habitat: Common through Portugal, central, southern and eastern Spain, on light soils and rocky open places.
Family: Compositae.

VIRGINIA STOCK

Malcomia maritima

Annual, low-spreading. Flowers bright mauve-violet, with prominent white or orange, square-shaped eye, petals four, 13-20mm across, broadly notched. Leaves oblong, entire or toothed. Fruits to 6cm long, covered with short adpressed hairs, shortly stalked. Sandy places, light soils and rocks, near the coast.
Habitat: Widespread, Spain to Greece and North Africa.
Family: Cruciferae.

VIRGIN'S BOWER

Clematis cirrhosa

A wiry-stemmed, very variable perennial shrub, sprawling and climbing over low bushes and shrubs. Readily distinguished by its dark evergreen, shiny leaves and conspicuous, large cream-yellow, nodding, bell-shaped flowers, occasionally red-spotted inside. Frequently cultivated for its attractive flowers. Flowering December to March.

Habitat: Widespread through Portugal and the European Mediterranean on scrubland, woodsides and the maquis.

Family: Ranunculaceae.

WHITE HENBANE

Hyocyamus albus

Spreading, coarse, variable biennial or perennial, 20-50cm high, glandular, hairy, often viscous. Leaves more or less egg-shaped, coarsely and irregularly lobed, greyish-green, upper often cordate. Flowers in lax racemes, large, pale greenish-yellow, one-sided above. Stamens short, protruding, filaments pale green. Very poisonous. Some authorities consider the brighter, yellow-flowered, black-purple-throated form a separate species, i.e. yellow henbane, H. aureus.

Habitat: Widespread low, coastal mountains Mediterranean area, on track sides, old walls and houses, rocky and waste places.

Family: Solanaceae.

WATER CROWFOOT

Ranunculus peltatus

A pretty annual or perennial, leaves both floating and submerged, covering up to 1m square. Submerged leaves long, filamentous, in clustered, diverging segments. Floating leaves, bright green, shiny, usually many, sometimes absent, reniform, strongly three to five-lobed, lobe ends shallowly cut, rounded. Flower usually profuse, up to 30mm wide, white, conspicuously yellow stamen, bossed, stamens 30, petals five sometimes more, margins usually touching. Fruit leaf opposing, on stalks as long as or longer than the leaf stalks. Some consider it a sub-species of R. aquatilis.
Habitat: Common in clear water throughout Europe to North Africa.
Family: Ranunculaceae.

WATER SPEEDWELL

Veronica anagallis-aquatica

Herb, upright, hairless annual or perennial, up to 30cm. Fairly readily recognised by its lax, wide, opposite-branching flowering stems and pale-blue flowers. Leaves, oval oblong, short-toothed and stalked, with rounded base. Stem and leaves a semi-succulent. Flowers four-petalled, pale blue 7-8mm wide, stamens exerted. Flower stems turn upwards after flowering.
Habitat: Europe, Asia, and almost worldwide in wet places, alongside streams, ponds and lake margins.
Family: Scrophulariaceae.

WATTLE, MIMOSA
Acacia cyanophylla

Small tree or bush to 6m high, immediately recognised by its long, blue-green, sharply basal narrowed, pendant leaves up to 30cm long and semi-pendant outer branches. Flowers abundant, borne in close, short clusters of three to five, resembling feathery, golden-yellow balls up to 1cm wide. Fruit pods constricted between the seeds. This and other species long cultivated for their showy flowers. A visual delight, early spring. For germination, mimosa seeds require immersing in boiling water overnight before sowing.
Habitat: A garden escape native to Western Australia, now widespread along the Mediterranean coast.
Family: Leguminosae.

WEASELS'S SNOUT
Antirrhinum orontium

Annual, stem erect, single or branched, up to 50cm, usually much smaller. Glandular, hairy above. Leaves pale green, entire, narrow linear, tapering at the base, lower opposite, upper alternate. Flowers small to 15mm long, pale pinkish-purple, borne in the axils of upper leaves to form a terminal leafy raceme. Calyx as long or longer than the corolla cut into narrow, linear, unequal lobes.
Habitat: Widespread, Europe, Mediterranean to the Himalayas, on cultivated, arable, wasteland, road and track sides.
Family: Scrophulariaceae.

WHITE ASPHODEL
Asphodelus albus

Handsome, tall, perennial, up to 1m high. Leaves greyish-green, long strap-like, broadly linear, channelled, narrowing to a point. Flowers held in tall, fairly dense spikes, the stem lengthening between maturing fruits, buds tightly packed. Tepals six, wide-spreading, star-like, white, meridian vein green, stamens and stigmas prominent. Bracts, blackish to very dark brown.
Habitat: Common on poor soils and rocky ground, Spain through the Mediterranean.
Family: Liliaceae.

WHITE BROOM
Lygos raetam

A deliciously fragrant, much-branched, generally leafless shrub up to 2m high, often less. Massed in close racemes of small pea-like white flowers up to 17mm long, late March to early April. Flowers ageing cream. Young branches, ridged, glabrous silvery, lateral branches pendulous. Fruit an oval-pointed, beaked pod up to 20mm long.
Habitat: Native to North Africa and Sicily, occasionally Spanish Mediterranean area, on light sandy soils in full sun.
Family: Leguminosae.

WHITE FLAX

Linum suffruticosum

Low-growing perennial but may under favourable conditions reach up to 50cm high. A linear dark-green-leaved sub-shrub, leaves rolled under at the sides, bristle-like, rough to the touch. Flowers large, white, conspicuous, buds pale yellow, petals often centred, crimson or violet with red markings at the base of the petals. Handsome when in flower, out of flower untidy-looking and easily missed.

Habitat: Common throughout the Mediterranean, on dry banks, hills, and roadsides.

Family: Linaceae.

WHITE-LEAVED BUGLOSS

Echium albicans

Attractive, silver-grey, haired perennial. Flower stems solitary, many up to 80cm high. Basal leaves silver, forming attractive rosettes, usually disappearing as flowering develops. Stem leaves similar, tapering linear. Flowers pink, or pink and blue together, on the same plant. Corolla open, bell-shaped, 2.5cm long. Calyx hairy, odd stamens often protruding.

Habitat: Endemic and local to a very small area of southern Spain on limestone soils.

Family: Boraginaceae.

WHITE MUSTARD
Sinapis alba

Lax-branched upright annual to 80cm high, glabrous, or more often pubescent, with downward-pointing hairs. Leaves stiff, hairy, up to 15cm long, pinnately lobed, the terrminal lobe larger than the lateral lobes. All leaves stalked. Flowers bright lemon-yellow, four-petalled, petals 10-15mm wide. Fruit up to 40mm long, with long beak. Seeds one to four.
Habitat: Widespread on calcareous soils, throughout Europe.
Family: Cruciferae.

31·03·09 - Conil

WHITE ROCK ROSE
Helianthemum apenninum

Attractive, conspicuous, white-flowered rock rose. A small, sprawling or ascending sub-shrub or clumpy plant, up to 30cm high, tips of branches frequently rooting. Leaves green to grey-green, revolute, hairy, more so below, oblong pointed to 3cm long. Flowers pure white to 2cm across, borne in loose clusters of 12 or less, centres marked five-star-like, chrome yellow. Calyx green-veined, veins frequently twisted on the unopened flower buds.
Habitat: Through the Mediterranean, the Alps and Pyrenees, on stony dry soils, in weak turf on hills and mountains.
Family: Cistaceae.

29·03·09 - AFP(P)
everywhere!

WHITE WATER-LILY

Nymphaea alba

A beautiful, easily recognised, still-water, deep-rooted, rhizomed aquatic plant. Leaves large circular, dark shining green above paler green or reddish-purple below. Fowers floating, very showy, white to 20cm across, petals generally 20 to 25 borne on submerged stems up to 3m long. Anthers contrasting yellow. Fruits generally submerging to ripen under water, released seeds float. The similar white-flowered N. Candida, native to northern Spain, has 15 to 18 petals with concave stigma.

Habitat: Ponds and lakes throughout Europe, but generally not southern Europe.

Family: Nymphaeaceae.

WILD CARROT

Daucus carota

A vigorous, hairy or non-hairy, variable, umbelliferous biennial, 30-100cm high. Umbels, white in broad, 3-7cm wide, many-rayed, usually flat or slightly concave heads, centred with one or more black-purple flowers. Umbels incurve conspicuously after flowering and when in fruit. Lower leaves long-stalked, feathery, upper more or less sessile, bract-like. Roots long, thin and tough. The sub-species, sativa, is the familiar culinary carrot.

Habitat: Widespread along the Mediterranean.

Family: Umbelliferae.

24.04.09 BEALO
26.04.09 AFP (P)

WILD CLARY
Salvia verbenaca

Variable perennial up to 50cm high, upper part hairy. Flowers pale to dark or purple-blue, usually open-mouthed, stigma protruding, held in close or spreading distinct whorls. Leaves opposite, lower stalked up to 10cm long, deeply cut, laciniated or rounded, coarsely rugose, ascending smaller up the stem and becoming stem-clasping.
Habitat: Common throughout the Mediterranean, fields, stony places, banks, hills, tracks, roadsides and screes.
Family: Labiatae.

WINTER WILD OAT
Avena sterilis

A vigorous, tall, annual oat, inflorescence lax, pendant on thin, wiry stalks, one-sided after flowering, spikelets wide-gaping, the two outer flowering glumes with long awns, the lowest hard, twisted, brown in colour. Leaves 15mm wide linear or linear lanceolate, with or without hairy margins. Ligules membraneous, 4-6mm long. One of the easier grasses to recognise due to its distinct resemblance to cultivated oats. The smaller similar "wild oat", A. ludoviciana, introduced into UK, is now a serious agricultural weed.
Habitat: Widespread on fields, waste areas, fallow ground, waysides and railway embankments.
Family: Gramineae.

WILD STRAWBERRY
Fragaria vesca

Perennial, rosetted herb, rootstock broadish and woody, producing long pale-green runners bearing small plants at the end, stipules reddish. Leaves ternate, leaflets toothed, bright green above, pale glaucous below, silky hairy. Flowers in small racemes, white, petals almost overlapping, held on stems just above the height of the leaves, up to 18mm across. Fruits, attractive, red, small 1-2cm wide, cone-shaped, edible, covered with small, straw-coloured achenes. Calyx spreading or reflexed.
Habitat: Widespread throughout Europe, in woodlands, shady places, on rich calcareous soils.
Family: Rosaceae.

WILLOW HERB
Epilobium duriaei

The smaller Epilobiums with their small, pale-coloured flowers and low stature tend to be insignificant. E. duriaei bears typical small flowers, 1-2mm wide, solitary, borne at the end of a long, usually pink-coloured, long, extended ovary. Petals four, pale pink, 6-10mm long. Stigma prominently four-lobed. Leaves, sessile, or short stalked, oval, soft green, irregularly toothed, with pointed ends, 15 to 35mm long.
Habitat: Mountains of northeast Spain, in shady moist areas.
Family: Onagraceae.

WOOD ANEMONE

Anemone nemorosa

Perennial, rhizomed herb, up to 30cm high often less, radical and stem leaves similar. Palmate three-lobed, the lobes further coarsely cut and divided. Flowers attractive, solitary, upward-facing, saucer-shaped, held above the stem leaves, white up to 4cm across, sometimes pinkish. Petals, up to nine, normally five to seven, stamens conspicuously clustered, golden yellow.

Habitat: Widespread Europe, western Asia, in damp deciduous woodland.

Family: Ranunculaceae.

YARROW, MILFOIL

Achillea millefolium

Aromatic, hairy, erect perennial, up to 60cm tall, usually less, patch forming on open land and often a weed in gardens. Leaves dark green, finely divided, fern-like, long lanceolate, 5 -12mm wide. Flowers in flat corymbs up to 10cm wide, white, sometimes pink or reddish-mauve. Rays (petals) usually five, short, bluntly three-toothed, veins three slightly depressed. Stigmas enclosed by very tiny campanulate five-petalled corollas, providing the flower heads with a very distinct appearance.

Habitat: Common throughout Europe, in dry fields, gardens, waste land, banks and roadsides. Rare through most of the Mediterranean.

Family: Compositae.

YELLOW ANEMONE
Anemone palmata

Distinguished by its soft hairy, palm-like leaves and large, 25-35mm-wide, bright-yellow-petalled, daisy-like flowers. Petals narrowly widening above, pointed, often copper flushed on the undersides. Height up to 30cm, usually much less. Leaf undersides frequently deep reddish to purple-tinged. Innocent-looking plant with poisonous properties.
Habitat: Common through Portugal, Spain into France, in damp places, in gullies, fields, rocky areas, fallow land and hillsides, often in shade.
Family: Ranunculaceae.

YELLOW BARTSIA
Parentucellia viscosa

Conspicuous, bright-yellow-flowered, semi-parasitic herb to 25cm high. Corolla two-lobed, the upper narrowly hooded, the lower, broadly three-lobed. Heads strongly borne in solitary terminal, dense spikes bearing broad-based, large, conspicuous, pointed, triangular to heart-shaped opposite, hairy bracts. Leaves narrow lanceolate, evenly toothed, sessile, medium green.
Habitat: Common, Europe, the Mediterranean and the Canary Islands in damp places, near lakes, streams, rivers.
Family: Scrophulariaceae.

YELLOW BEE ORCHID
Ophrys lutea

Perennial, readily distinguished by its three to six conspicuous yellow flowers, borne on stems usually leafless at the flowering period, up to 30cm tall. Lip black-brown, with two large, ovoid, deep blue-black, shiny patches at the top, the surround outward-flared, dull to bright yellow, lobes with three indents. Pollinated by a small wasp — males unwittingly pollinate the flower as the plant resembles and smells like the female wasp.
Habitat: Common in the Mediterranean area, on sparse grass, banks, rocky areas, tracks and roadsides.
Family: Orchidaceae.

YELLOW FUMITORY
Corydalis lutea

Perennial herb up to 30cm high. Readily identified by its medium heads of conspicuous, outward-facing, lemon-yellow flowers and blue-green two to three times pinnate, fern-like leaves, with stalked leaflets. Flowers, 12-18mm long, held closely, six to 16 in leaf-opposed clusters. Petals yellow, the upper petal with short, blunt, downward-pointing spur, tube whitish. Leaves long-stalked, glaucous.
Habitat: Europe, central and eastern Spain, on rocks, old walls and bridges in shady places.
Family: Fumariaceae.

YELLOW LOOSESTRIFE
Lysimachia vulgaris

Conspicuous,readilydistinguished, very bright, yellow, attractively flowered, upright perennial, softly hairy thoughout. Leaves yellow-green, in whorls of three to four, or borne opposite, to 9cm, long, oval lanceolate. Flowers up to 20mm wide, profuse, held three to four in the leaf axils, upwards on long, branching terminal spikes.
Habitat: Wet areas, pond and lake sides and marshes, widespread in most of central Europe, including central Spain northwards, absent from the south.
Family: Primulaceae.

YELLOW KNAPWEED
Centaurea granatensis

Easily recognised by its hard knapweed heads, buds of overall whitish appearance and large, bright yellow, thistle-like, slightly spiny, bracted flowers, up to 3cm across. These usually borne solitary on sparsely leaved stems 30 to 50cm tall. Flower and bracts ends brown and pointed.
Habitat: Found in stony banks and hills, southern Spain.
Family: Compositae.

YELLOW PIMPERNEL
Lysimachia nemorum

Easily recognised creeping perennial with softly hairy, pale-green, broad oval-pointed leaves, to 30cm long, veins weak to strongly indented. Flowers borne singly from the leaf axils, bright yellow, to about 12mm wide, petals five, divided to the base, stamens slender, almost as long as the petals.
Habitat: Common throughout northern Spain, west and central Europe, in damp, shady places, woodlands and hedgerows.
Family: Primulaceae.

YELLOW RATTLE
Rhinanthus major

A very difficult-to-identify genus, hybridising readily between the species into a number of sub-species. Annual, sometimes tall, up to 28cm high, very variable, the yellow greenish to whitish bracts are to some extent diagnostic. Flowers yellow, mouth usually closed, about 2cm long, upper lip small with two small violet-coloured teeth. Calyx hairy, ribbed. Leaves pale green, toothed lanceolate, up to 7cm long.
Habitat: Widespread throughout the mountainous areas of Europe, ascending to 2,500m.
Family: Scrophulariaceae.

YELLOW WORT

Blackstonia perfoliata

Bright, appealing yellow star-flowered, erect annual. Glaucous, up to 45cm high, often less, basal leaves rosetted. Stem usually branched above. Leaves, oval, opposite, lower free, the upper usually united or fused to encircle the stem. Flowers bright yellow, six to eight-petalled, carried in lax cyme, 8-15mm wide.

Habitat: Widespread through Europe, in light soils, fields, sands and dunes. A smaller flowered form occurs in eastern Spain.

Family: Gentianaceae.

EXOTIC PLANTS

Widely cultivated throughout the Mediterranean, the exotic plants illustrated are classed by some authorities as wild flowers. A brief description is therefore included.

SEVILLE ORANGE

Citrus aurantium

Flowers white, highly perfumed, February. Colourful Christmas-fruiting, roadside tree.

JAPANESE LOQUAT

Eriobotrya japonica

Small evergreen tree, leaves large, rough, fruits pale orange, edible, plum-size.

SUCCULENT
Aloe arboreum

Flowers December, red-hot-poker-like, pollinated by birds, sometimes mistaken for Aloe vera which has upright leaves and yellow flowers.

FLAME VINE
Pyrostegia venusta

Brilliantly vermilion-coloured, vigorous climber over walls and fences, December.

ANGEL'S TRUMPET
Datura suaveolens

Shrub, leaves large soft, flowers white, fragrant, pendant, 22cm-long trumpets.

PINK TRUMPET VINE
Bignonia rosea

Well-known vigorous climber, with clusters of wide-mouthed, rosy pink, fragrant, trumpet-like flowers.

GUIDE TO PLANT NAMES

ENGLISH	*LATIN*	SPANISH
Alkanet	Anchusa	Lengua de buey, Lenguaza
Almond	Prunas dulcis	Almendro
Annual toadflax	Linaria vulgaris	Linaria
Asparagus	Asparagus	Esparraguera
Autumn buttercup	Ranunculus bullatus	Flor de San Diego
Autumn crocus	Colchicum autumnale	Cólchico
Autumn snowflake	Leucojum autumnale	Campanilla
Barbary nut	Iris sissyrinchium	Lirio
Bindweed	Convolvulus	Corregüela menor
Bear's breech	Acanthus mollis	Acanto, Alas de angel
Broom rape	Orobanche crenata	Rabo de lobo
Beautiful flax	Linum narbonense	Lino bravo
Bermuda buttercup	Oxalis pes-caprae	Vinagrera
Bee orchid	Ophrys apifera	Abejera
Biennial cornflower	Centaurea pullata	Centaurea
Bladder campion	Silene vulgaris	Silene. Colleja
Broom	Genista sphaerocarpa, syn. Lygos sphaerocarpa	Retama macho
Candytuft	Iberis crenata	Carraspique
Carlina	Carlina vulgaris	Cardo de la uva
Carob tree	Ceratonia siliqua	Algarrobo
Carthamus	Carthamus arborescens	Cardo cabrero
Century plant	Agave americana	Pita
Chaste tree	Vitis agnus-castus	Agnocasto, Gatillo casto
Chicory	Cichorium intybus	Achicoria
Christmas iris, Wide-leaved iris	Iris planifolia	Lirio
Chrysanthemum (Crown daisy)	Chrysanthemum coronarium	Mirabeles, Parajito
Cistus	Cistus crispus	Jara, Jaguarzo
Cocklebur	Xanthium	Bardana menor
Common centaury	Centaurium erythraea	Hiel de la tierra, Centaura menor
Common mallow	Malva sylvestris	Malva común
Common milkwort	Polygala serpyllifolia	Poligala, Hierba lechera

ENGLISH	*LATIN*	SPANISH
Common poppy, Field poppy,	Papaver rhoeas	Amapola
Common toadflax	Linaria vulgaris	Linaria
Common grapevine	Vitis vinifera	Vid, parra
Corn marigold	Chrysanthemum segetum	Pajitos
Common smilax	Smilax aspera	Zarzaparilla
Corsican heath	Erica terminalis	Brezo
Crocus	Crocus serotinus	Azafrán
Creeping Jenny	Lysimachia nummularia	Hierba de la moneda
Cupidone	Catanache	Hierba cúpida
Curry plant, everlasting	Helichrysum stoechas	Siempreviva
Cut-leaved lavender	Lavandula multifida	Alhucemilla
Cytinus	Cytinus hypocistus	Doncella
Daffodil	Narcissus hispanicus	Narciso
Daisy	Bellis	Margarita
Danewort	Sambucus ebulus	Yezgo
Daphne	Daphne gnidium	Torvisco
Dutchman's pipe, Birthwort	Aristolochia baetica	Candiles
English lavender	Lavendula angustifolia	Espliego
Etruscan Honeysuckle	Lonicera etrusca	Madreselva
Evening primrose	Oenothera	Hierba del asno
Everlasting pea	Lathyrus latifolius	Alverjana
Feddia	Feddia cornucopiae	Lechuguilla de la Alcarría
Forget-me-not tree	Wigandia caracasana	Wigandia
Foxglove	Digitalis purpurea	Calzones de Zora
Fragrant bug orchid	Orchis coriophora, Ssp. fragrans	Orquídea
French lavender	Lavandula stoechas	Cantueso, Azaya
Fringed rue	Ruta chalepensis	Ruda
Genista	Genista sphaerocarpa	Retama, Retama macho
Genista	Genista hirsuta	Aulaga
Giant fennel	Ferula communis	Cañaferla, Cañaheja
Giant thapsia	Thapsia garganica	Tapsia, Asa dulce
Gladiolus	Gladiolus communis	Gladiolo
Goatsbeard	Tragopogon hybridum	Barba cabruna
Grape hyacinth	Muscari neglectum	Jacinto de penacho
Green stonecrop	Sedum sediforme	Uvas de pájaro

ENGLISH	*LATIN*	SPANISH
Grey-leaved sunrose	Cistus albidus	Jara estepa
Gum cistus	Cistus ladaniferus	Jara pringosa
Hairy lupin	Lupinus micranthus	Altramuz
Hawthorn	Crataegus	Espino
Hemlock	Conium maculatum	Ceguta
Hoary mullein	Verbascum pulverulentum	Gordolobo
Hollow-stemmed asphodel	Asphodelus fistulosus	Gamón
Holm oak	Quercus ilex	Encina, Carrasca
Hottentot fig	Carpobrotus	Flor de cuchillo
Hound's tongue	Cynoglossum	Cinoglosa
Large yellow rest harrow	Ononis natrix	Beluda, Pegamoscas
Laurestinus	Viburnum tinus	Durillo
Lesser celandine	Ranunculus ficaria, v. Grandiflora	Celidonia menor
Lizard orchid	Himantoglossum hircinum	Orquídea
Loose-leaved orchid	Orchis laxiflora	Orquídea
Long-leaved helleborine	Cephalanthera longifolia	Orquídea
Lupin	Lupinus	Altramuz
Mandrake	Mandragora autumnalis	Mandrágora
Maritime pine	Pinus pinaster	Pino
Milk thistle	Silybum marianum	Lechero
Myrtle	Myrtus communis	Mirto común, Murta
Naked ladies	Colchicum lusitanicum	Colchico
Naked man orchid	Orchis italica	Orquídea
Narcissus	Narcissus serotinus	Narciso
Oleander	Nerium oleander	Adelfa
Orchid	Orchis mascula	Orquídea
Paperwhite Narcissus	Narcissus papyraceus	Narciso
Paronychia	Paronychia capitata	Arrecadas
Pennyroyal	Mentha pulegium	Poleo
Peony	Paeonia broteroi	Rosa de rejalgar, Peonía
Peruvian squill	Scilla peruviana	Albarrana
Phlomis	Phlomis crinita	Aguavientos
Phlomis	Phlomis lychnitis	Candilera, Torcida de candil
Phlomis	Phlomis purpurea	Matagallo

ENGLISH	*LATIN*	SPANISH
Pink butterfly orchid	Orchis papilionacea	Orquídea
Plantain	Plantago lagopus	Lengua de perro
Pomegranate tree	Punica granatum	Granado
Prickly pear, Barbary fig	Opuntia Ficus-indica	Chumbera
Provence orchid	Orchis provincialis	Orquídea
Putoria	Putoria calabrica	Hedionda
Quaking grass	Briza maxima	Bailarines, Tembladera
Red-berried mistletoe	Viscum cruciatum	Marojo, Muérdago
Rosemary	Rosemarinus officinalis	Romero
Rush-leaved jonquil	Narcissus juncifolius	Narciso
Sand Spurrey	Spergularia rubra	Vermella
Sawfly orchid	Ophrys tenthredinifera	Orquídea
Sea daffodil	Pancratium maritimum	Nardo marino
Sea lavender	Limonium sinuatum	Acelga silvestre
Self heal	Prunilla vulgaris	Hierba de las heridas
Sea squill	Urginea maritima	Cebolla albarrana, Esquila
Shrubby pimpernel	Anagallis monelli	Murajes de lino
Small-flowered gorse, furze	Ulex parviflorus	Aulaga morena, Tojo
Small-flowered tongue orchid	Serapius pseudocordigera	Serapia
Snapdragon	Antirrhinum granatum	Boca de dragón blanco
Snapdragon	Antirrhinum majus	Boca de dragón
Sombre bee orchid, dull orchid	Ophrys fusca	Orquídea
Southern vetchling	Lathyrus tingitanus	Alverjana de tanger
Spanish broom	Spartium junceum	Retama de olor
Spanish iris	Iris Xiphium	Lirio de España
Spanish rusty foxglove	Digitalis obscura	Dedalera. Crujia
Spotted orchid	Dactylorhiza maculata	Orquídea
Spurge laurel	Daphne laureola	Adelfilla, Laureola común
Squirting cucumber	Ecballium elaterium	Cohombrillo amargo, Pepinillo del diablo
Star thistle	Centaurea calcitrapa	Cardo estrellado
Stonecrop, Wall pepper	Sedum acre	Uvas de gato
Sweet chestnut	Castanea sativa	Castaño

ENGLISH	*LATIN*	SPANISH
Tamarix	Tamarix hispanica	Taray, Atarce
Teasel	Dipsacus fullonum	Cardencha,
Tassel hyacinth	Muscari comosum	Jacinto de penacho
Thistle, Common thistle	Galactites tomentosa	Cardo común
Thorny broom	Calycotome infesta	Erguenes
Throatwort	Trachelium caeruleum	Flor de viuda, Hermosilla
Thyme (Andalucian or Shrubby)	Thymus capitatus	Tomillo común
Touch-me-not, Balsam	Impatiens	Hierba de Santa Catalina
Tree germander	Teucrium fruticans	Olivilla
Tree heath	Erica arborea	Brezo blanco, Urce,
Turpentine tree	Pistacia terebinthus	Terebinto
Viper's grass	Scorzonera crispatula	Escorzonera, Cornicabra
Wattle, Mimosa	Acacia cyanophylla	Acacia, Mimosa
White asphodel	Asphodelus albus	Gamón
White flax	Linum suffruticosum	Hierba sanjuana, Lino blanco,
White henbane	Hycoyamus albus	Beleño
White-leaved bugloss	Echium albicans	Viborera
Wild carrot	Daucus carota	Zanahoria silvestre
Wood anemone	Anemone nemorosa	Anemone
Yarrow, Millfoil	Achillea millefolium	Milefolio
Yellow anemone	Anemone palmata	Hierba centella
Yellow bee orchid	Ophrys lutea	Flor de abeja amarilla, Abejera
Yellow loosetrife	Lysimachia vulgaris	Lysimaquia amarilla

GLOSSARY

Abbreviations

Var: variety. Syn: synonymous. Ssp: Sub-species.

Plant habitats

Garique: Low, soft-leafed scrubland on limestone soils around the Mediterranean basin, generally near the coast.
Maquis: Dense thickets of shrubs 1-3m high and covering wide areas.
Littoral: Area lying along the coast.

Achene: Single-fruited, non-splitting seed, e.g. buttercups, strawberry seeds.
Acuminate: Tapering to a point.
Adpressed: Leaves all held strongly flat and rigid against the ground supressing other plant growth and avoiding grazing by stock, or hairs pressed hard and flat against the leaves or stems.
Anther: Pollen-bearing part of stamen, usually at the tip.
Awn: Usually related to grasses, the stiff bristle-like projection rising from the back of the lemma or from the tip of the stigma, e.g. in *Erodium*, and sometimes a reference to a leaf tip.

Berry: A fleshy fruit without any surrounding stony layer, often several seeded.
Biennial: A plant flowering in the second year rather than the first in order to complete its life cycle.
Bifid: Deeply split into two.
Bract: Small leaf or very small leaf-like structures above the normal leaves but below the flowers.
Bulb: Underground swollen organ consisting of embryo plant covered and surrounded by swollen, fleshy scale leaves, e.g. daffodil.
Bulbil: Immature bulb, usually arising in flowering inflorescence or leaf axils, vegetatively replacing seeds.

Calcifuge: Plants disliking and usually not thriving on limy and chalky soils.
Calyx: The sepals, usually green, below a flower's brightly coloured petals.
Campanulate: In the shape of a bell.
Capsule: Dry-splitting, seed-bearing fruit, of more than one carpel.
Carpel: A unit division of the ovary, separate, joined or fused.

Chromosomes: Very small paired bodies, containing the organism's inherent qualities within the cell nuclei.
Contiguous: Parts touching each other.
Cordate: Heart-shaped at base.
Corm: Swollen short, usually upright, underground annual stem, newly formed each year above the old, exhausted corm, e.g. crocus.
Corolla: Petals separate or fused together.
Corona: Central, separate, cup-like rim of a flower, e.g. daffodil.
Corymb: Raceme with the flowers forming a flat (or almost flat), sometimes dense head, e.g. yarrow.
Crenate: Rounded teeth of leaf margins

Decurrent: Leaf base continuing narrow-wing-like down the stem.
Drupe: Fleshy fruit with stone or stones surrounded by a hard woody layer e.g. cherry, plum.

Elliptic: Ellipse shape

Filiform: Thin thread-like.
Filament: The stalk of the pollen-bearing anthers.

Genus: A group of closely related plants within a family. The first name of the family, followed by the species and the member of that group, e.g. *Iris xipheum*, I. germanica, I. planifolia. The generic (group) name always commences with a capital letter, the specific name with a small letter.
Glabrous: Smooth, hairless.
Gland: Small globular or oval protuberance of the plant, let into or on the surface of leaves or stems, usually oil or resin-bearing. When held on a slender hair, known as a glandular hair.
Glandular: Gland-possessing.
Glaucous: Green-blue colour, e.g. opium poppy.
Glume: Two dry bracts enclosing the young spikelets of grass flower heads

Hastate: Arrow-head-shaped
Herb: A none-woody plant
Hispid: Bristly hairy.

Inflorescence: Flowering portion of the stem above the last stem leaves.
Involucre: Small leaf-like structures below a flower head, e.g. common daisy. Consisting of the usually close-covering involucral bracts.

Keel: Two, often forward-pointing petals pushed outwards together in the form of the keel of a boat, e.g. sweet pea.

Labellum: The large conspicuous frontal, usually lower, lip, often brightly coloured in orchids.
Laciniate: Deep, irregularly divided, narrow segments, usually of leaves.
Lanceolate: Lance-shaped.
Lemma: Two small bracts enclosing and forming a grass floret (sometimes absent) the upper thin and delicate, the lower coriaceous (leathery).
Ligule: The membraneous bracts of grass stems, also of some daisies.
Linear: Thin and narrow.
Local: Plant may be abundant but in limited or isolated areas.

Node: The place in the stem where leaves arise, in some plants swollen.

Ovary: The fertile (fruit, seed-bearing) organ of the plant.
Ovate: Oval, base often cordate (heart-shaped).

Palmate: More than three leaflets arising from one point, (hand, palm-like).
Panicle: A branched inflorescence (correctly applied only to a branched racemose inflorescence) but generally broadly applied.
Perfoliate: Used to describe a leaf completely encircling the stem, e.g. honeysuckle, some juvenile Eucalyptus.
Perianth: The floral "leaves" (both sepals and petals), especially when not easily separated e.g. *Narcissi*.
Petal: A part of the brightly coloured, inner series of the perianth, if differing from the outer.
Petiole: Leaf stalk.
Phyllode: A modified, leaf-like stalk or stem, usually flattened, functioning as and replacing the true leaves, e.g. *Parkinsonia*.
Pinnate: The blade of a leaf divided or cut into segments deep to the mid-rib, bipinnate and tripinnate (meaning twice or three times cut).
Pubescent: Short and softly haired, or softly hairy.

Raceme: Unbranched flowering stem, flowers single-stalked, usually opening from the base upwards.
Ray: The stalk of a partial umbel, the narrow petals (ray florets) of a flower, e.g. daisy.
Reniform: Shaped in the form of a kidney.
Reticulate: Netted or marked, usually with veins.
Rhizome: Underground stem bearing roots and shoots.

Scabrid: Rough, especially to the touch.
Scrub or thicket: Community of plants dominated by shrubs.
Serrate: Leaf margins toothed, saw-like.
Sessile: Without (leaf) stalks.
Shrub: Woody perennial plant often tall and wide spreading.
Spathe: A large, often leaf-like, coloured bract enclosing the flowers, e.g. *arum*.
Spathulate: Paddle or spoon-shaped, spatular.
Spike: A simple raceme, flowers unstalked.
Spur: Hollow, slender, often cone-like projection from the corolla, or petals.
Stamen: Male, pollen-bearing organ.
Standard: The largest upright petal, usually at the back of the flower, e.g. sweet pea.
Stigma: The receptive female organ, usually at the top of the style and slightly sticky.
Stipule: Usually small, scale or leaf-like appendages at the base of the leaf stalk.
Stoloniferous: Having a stem or branch that takes root points along its length.
Style: A slender stem, generally above and connecting the stigma (female organ) to the ovary.

Tessellated: Checkered
Thorn: Woody, sharp, modified branch.
Tomentose: Thick woolly or cottony-haired.
Triquetrous: Of triangular section.
Tunic: Dry papery "skin", outer covering of a bulb or corm, e.g. Colchicum, tulip.

Umbel: A compound flower, all the stems (pedicels) arise from the same point, usually the top of a single stem, umbrella-like.

Villous: Shaggy
Viscid: Sticky

Whorl: Two or more organs of the same kind arising from the same point of the stem, e.g. penny royal.

Xerophytic: A plant adapted and resistant to drought, e.g. cacti, pines.

BIBLIOGRAPHY

Anthony Huxley, **Mountain Flowers**, Blandford Press, 1967.
Betty Molesworth Allen, **A selection of Wildflowers of Southern Spain**, Mirador, Spain, 1993.
Bob Press and Bob Gibbons, **Wild Flowers of Britain and Europe**, New Holland Publishers, UK, 1993.
Clapham, Tutin and Warburg, **Flora of the British Isles,** Cambridge University Press,1952.
Marjorie Belamey and Christopher Grey-Wilson, **Wild Flowers of the Mediterranean,** A.C. Black, London, 2004.
Oleg Polunin and Anthony Huxley, **Flowers of the Mediterranean,** Chatto and Windus, London, 1981.
Also informative re climate and land habitats.
Oleg Polunin and B.E. Smythies, **Flowers of South -West Europe,** Oxford University Press, 1973. Includes geological habitat and land form surveys.